My **BIBLE NOW!**

_____

With love from

_____

_on_

_____

BIBLE NOW!

101 Amazing Stories for Today's Young Readers

Contemporary English Version

AMERICAN BIBLE SOCIETY

BIBLE NOW!
101 Amazing Stories for Today's Young Readers
adapted from the *Contemporary English Version*

This is a Portion of Holy Scripture adapted from the *Contemporary English Version*. American Bible Society is a not-for-profit organization which publishes the Scriptures without doctrinal note or comment. Since 1816, its single mission is to make the Bible available to every person in a language and format each can understand and afford. Working toward this goal American Bible Society is a member of the United Bible Societies, a worldwide effort that extends to more than 200 countries and territories. You are urged to read the Bible and to share it with others. For information on other Scripture publications, call American Bible Society at 1-800-32-BIBLE, or write to 101 North Independence Mall E., FL8, Philadelphia, PA 19106. Visit the American Bible Society website: **www.americanbible.org.**

Illustrated by Paul and Delores Gully
Editors Larry Keefauver, Steve Berneking, Adina Hamik, and Charles Houser

ISBN 978-1-941448-56-4

Preface

Everybody loves a good story! And the Bible is filled with stories about God and the special relationship God has with people.

Bible Now! was developed with your child in mind. The 101 stories represent the most important and foundational ones found in the Old and New Testaments. Many others could have been selected. But after reading these stories, your child will have learned about the central characters of the Bible, as well as some of the key events and places of the biblical world.

Each story has three central components.

- First, the story is told in easy-to-understand words that come from a modern English Bible translation: the *Contemporary English Version* (CEV), published by the American Bible Society (1995). If you compare each story in ***Bible Now!*** with those in the full CEV Bible, you may notice a few differences. Some changes were made to ensure that the story is both easy to read (for your readers) and easy to hear (for your non-readers).

In some cases, difficult place names were omitted, details not essential to the story line were deleted, and necessary information needed for comprehension was added. In some instances, when details were needed to put the story in a clearer context, one or two sentences were added to prepare the reader-hearer for the story. You will see that such details are set in italics to indicate that they are not Scripture.

- Second, there is a Key Verse that represents a central part of the story. This Verse may repeat an important declaration of a character, a major turning point or peak in the plot, or a significant teaching from the story. While the Key Verse may sometimes be too long to be memorized by your child, it certainly can be used as an aid to help a child reflect on an important aspect of the biblical text.

- Third, each story is illustrated with colorful drawings with captions. These

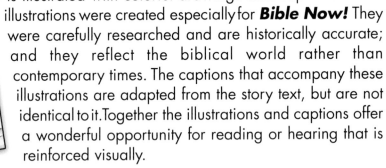

illustrations were created especially for **Bible Now!** They were carefully researched and are historically accurate; and they reflect the biblical world rather than contemporary times. The captions that accompany these illustrations are adapted from the story text, but are not identical to it. Together the illustrations and captions offer a wonderful opportunity for reading or hearing that is reinforced visually.

In addition, **Bible Now!** contains a number of helpful resources. The four maps set the stage for the stories, the timeline teaches the relationship between characters and events, and the glossary explains places and concepts your child will encounter in the Bible. Finally, the three indices at the back of the book will help you locate stories based on names, themes, and Scripture passages.

Spend time getting to know the many features of **Bible Now!** Spend time reading it to your child. Spend time listening to your child read it to you. And spend time talking with your child about these Bible stories and what we learn from them about God and about ourselves.

Table of Contents

Page 16

Page 24

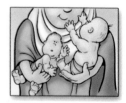

Page 48

Page 96

Page 120

Page 148

Page 156

Page 196

Page 200

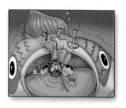

Page 240

New Testament

Page 254

Page 266

Page 298

Page 330

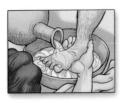

Page 342

Page 370

Page 386

Page 425

Page 438

My Reading Toolbox

Welcome to
Bible Now!
101 Amazing Stories for Today's Young Readers

Bible Now! has some very exciting stories to tell. These stories are about God and the people who love God. There are over 100 stories in this Bible, and each one of them has great pictures that you can read from as well.

Bible Now! has two parts to it: an Old Testament and a New Testament. Some of the people you will meet in the Old Testament are Noah, Abraham, Moses and Ruth. They were brave leaders who wanted to obey God and do the right thing to help others.

Many of the stories you will read in the New Testament are about Jesus—what he said and did to show God's love to everyone. You will also meet Mary and Joseph, and people like Peter and Paul who wanted to tell everyone about what Jesus had done for them and for others.

Read your *Bible Now!* over and over to learn more about God's love and how God wants us all to act. Read it with your friends and read it to the adults you know. The stories in *Bible Now!* are ones you will remember your entire life.

Old Testament

God Creates the World

In the beginning God created the heavens and the earth. The earth was barren, with no form of life; it was under a roaring ocean covered with darkness. But the Spirit of God was moving over the water.

The First Day—God said, "I command light to shine!" And light started shining.

The Second Day—God said, "I command a dome to separate the water above it from the water below it." And that's what happened.

The Third Day—God said, "I command the water under the sky to come together in one place, so there will be dry ground." And that's what happened. And God said, "I command the earth to produce all kinds of plants, including fruit trees and grain." And that's what happened.

The Fourth Day—God said, "I command lights to appear in the sky and to separate day from night and to show the time for seasons, special days, and years. I command them to shine on the earth." And that's what happened.

The Fifth Day—God said, "I command the ocean to be full of living creatures, and I command birds to fly above the earth." So God made all the living creatures that swim in the ocean and every kind of bird.

The Sixth Day—God said, "I command the earth to give life to all kinds of tame animals, wild animals, and reptiles." And that's what happened.

Then God said, "Now we will make humans, and they will be like us. We will let them rule the fish, the birds, and all other living creatures." So God created humans to be like himself. God looked at what he had done. All of it was very good! So the heavens and the earth and everything else were created.

The Seventh Day—By the seventh day, God had finished his work, and so he rested. God blessed the seventh day and made it special because on that day he rested from his work.

That's how God created the heavens and the earth.

Based on Genesis 1.1–2.4

In the beginning God created the heavens and the earth.

In the beginning God created the heavens and the earth.

On the first day, God created light.
God named the light "day" and the darkness "night."

On the second day, God created a dome to separate the water above from the water below. God named the dome "sky."

On the third day, God separated the water from dry ground. And God named the dry ground "land."

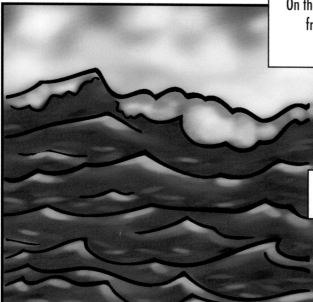

God named the water "ocean."

God created all kinds of plants, including fruit trees and grain.

On the fourth day, God made the sun to shine during the day.

And God made the moon to shine during the night. God also made the stars.

On the fifth day, God created all the fish and sea creatures that swim in the ocean.

Also on the fifth day, God made the birds that fly in the sky.

On the sixth day, God created all animals that move on dry land.

Also on the sixth day, God said, "We will make humans to be like us!" God made man and woman and blessed them, saying, "Have a lot of children!"

God looked at all he had created and saw that it was very good!

Life in God's Garden

When the LORD God made the heavens and the earth, no grass or plants were growing anywhere. God had not yet sent any rain, and there was no one to work the land. But streams came up from the ground and watered the earth.

The LORD God took a handful of soil and made a man. God breathed life into the man, and the man started breathing. The LORD made a garden in a place called Eden, which was in the east, and he put the man there.

The LORD God placed all kinds of beautiful trees and fruit trees in the garden. Two other trees were in the middle of the garden. One of the trees gave life—the other gave the power to know the difference between right and wrong.

The LORD God put the man in the Garden of Eden to take care of it and to look after it. But the LORD told him, "You may eat fruit from any tree in the garden, except the one that has the power to let you know the difference between right and wrong. If you eat any fruit from that tree, you will die before the day is over!"

The LORD God said, "It isn't good for the man to live alone. I need to make a suitable partner for him." So the LORD took some soil and made animals and birds. He brought them to the man to see what names he would give each of them. Then the man named the tame animals and the birds and the wild animals. That's how they got their names.

None of these was the right kind of partner for the man. So the LORD God made him fall into a deep sleep, and he took out one of the man's ribs. Then after closing the man's side, the LORD made a woman out of the rib.

The LORD God brought her to the man, and the man exclaimed, "Here is someone like me! She is part of my body, my own flesh and bones. She came from me, a man. So I will name her Woman!"

Although the man and his wife were both naked, they were not ashamed.

Based on Genesis 2.4-25

God breathed life into the man, and the man started breathing.

God made a man from the ground.

God breathed life into the man, and the man started breathing.

God made a beautiful garden and planted two trees.

"Do not eat from the tree that gives knowledge."

God made animals so the man would not be alone.

God created a partner for the man.

The man named her Woman.

15

Adam and Eve Make a Bad Choice

The snake was sneakier than any of the other wild animals that the LORD God had made. One day it came to the woman and asked, "Did God tell you not to eat fruit from any tree in the garden?"

The woman answered, "God said we could eat fruit from any tree in the garden, except the one in the middle. God told us not to eat fruit from that tree or even to touch it. If we do, we will die."

"No, you won't!" the snake replied. "God understands what will happen on the day you eat fruit from that tree. You will see what you have done, and you will know the difference between right and wrong, just as God does."

The woman wanted the wisdom that the fruit would give her, and she ate some of the fruit. Her husband was there with her, so she gave some to him, and he ate it too. Right away they saw what they had done, and they realized they were naked. Then they sewed fig leaves together to make something to cover themselves.

The LORD called out to the man and asked, "Where are you?"

The man answered, "I was naked, and when I heard you walking through the garden, I was frightened and hid!"

"How did you know you were naked?" God asked. "Did you eat any fruit from that tree in the middle of the garden?"

"It was the woman you put here with me," the man said. "She gave me some of the fruit, and I ate it."

The LORD God then asked the woman, "What have you done?"

"The snake tricked me," she answered. "And I ate some of that fruit."

Then the LORD God made clothes out of animal skins for the man and his wife. The LORD said, "These people now know the difference between right and wrong, just as we do. But they must not be allowed to eat fruit from the tree that lets them live forever." So the LORD God sent them out of the Garden of Eden, where they would have to work the ground from which the man had been made.

Based on Genesis 3.1-24

The woman answered, "God said we could eat fruit from any tree in the garden, except the one in the middle."

Adam and Eve lived in Eden with the animals and the snake.

"Can you eat the fruit from any tree?"

"God told us, we cannot eat from that one special tree."

The woman ate the fruit and gave some to the man.

Jealousy Leads to Trouble

Adam and Eve had a son. Then Eve said, "I'll name him Cain because I got him with the help of the LORD." Later she had another son and named him Abel.

Abel became a sheep farmer, but Cain farmed the land. One day, Cain gave part of his harvest to the LORD, and Abel also gave an offering to the LORD. He killed the first-born lamb from one of his sheep and gave the LORD the best parts of it. The LORD was pleased with Abel and his offering, but not with Cain and his offering. This made Cain so angry that he could not hide his feelings.

The LORD said to Cain, "What's wrong with you? Why do you have such an angry look on your face? Sin wants to destroy you, but don't let it!"

Cain said to his brother Abel, "Let's go for a walk." And when they were out in a field, Cain killed him. Afterwards the LORD asked Cain, "Where is Abel?"

"How should I know?" Cain answered. "Am I supposed to look after my brother?"

Then the LORD said, "Why have you done this terrible thing? You killed your own brother. Because you killed Abel, you will never be able to farm the land again. From now on, you'll be without a home, and you'll spend the rest of your life wandering from place to place."

Based on Genesis 4.1-16

The LORD asked Cain, "Where is Abel?"
"How should I know?" he answered.
"Am I supposed to look after my brother?"

Adam and Eve had two sons.

Abel raised sheep. Cain farmed the land.

The LORD was pleased with Abel's offering.

The LORD was not pleased with Cain's offering.

Cain became angry.

God said, "Don't get too angry."

Cain killed his brother.

"Do I need to watch over my brother?"

God was disappointed
and sent Cain away.

Cain spent his life wandering.

Noah Builds a Big Boat

The LORD saw how bad the people on earth were and that everything they thought and planned was evil. He was very sorry that he had made them, and he said, "I'll destroy every living creature on earth!" But the LORD was pleased with Noah. Noah was the only person who lived right and obeyed God.

God knew that everyone was terribly cruel and violent. So he told Noah: "Cruelty and violence have spread everywhere. Now I'm going to destroy the whole earth and its entire people. Get some good lumber and build a boat. Put rooms in it and cover it with tar inside and out.

"I'm going to send a flood that will destroy everything that breathes! But I solemnly promise that you, your wife, your sons, and your daughters-in-law will be kept safe in the boat.

"Bring into the boat with you a male and a female of every kind of animal and bird, as well as a male and a female of every reptile. I don't want them to be destroyed. Store up enough food both for yourself and for them." Noah did everything the LORD told him to do.

Noah's wife, his sons, and his daughters-in-law all went inside the boat with him. He obeyed God and took a male and a female of each kind of animal and bird into the boat with him. Seven days later a flood began to cover the earth.

For forty days the rain poured down without stopping. And the water became deeper and deeper, until the boat started floating high above the ground. Finally, the mighty flood was so deep that even the highest mountain peaks were almost twenty-five feet below the surface of the water. Not a bird, animal, reptile, or human was left alive anywhere on earth. Nothing was left alive except Noah and the others in the boat. A hundred fifty days later, the water started going down.

About one year later, all the water had gone down, and the earth was completely dry.

God said to Noah, "You, your wife, your sons, and your daughters-in-law may now leave the boat. Let out the birds, animals, and reptiles, so they can mate and live all over the earth."

God said to Noah and his sons, "I am giving you my blessing. Have a lot of children and grandchildren, so people will live everywhere on this earth. I am going to make a solemn promise to you and to everyone who will live after you. This includes the birds and the animals that came out of the boat. I promise every living creature that the earth and those living on it will never again be destroyed by a flood. The rainbow that I have put in the sky will be my sign to you and to every living creature on earth. It will remind you that I will keep this promise forever."

Based on Genesis 6–9

God said, "When I see the rainbow in the sky, I will always remember the promise that I have made to every living creature."

God was angry because people did bad things.

God decided to send a flood, but save Noah and his family.

God told Noah to build a boat.

Noah's family and animals came onto the boat.

The flood covered the earth.

Noah, his family, and the animals were saved.

The rainbow means God will never flood the earth again.

Let's Build a Tower to Heaven!

At first everyone spoke the same language, but after some of them moved from the east and settled in Babylonia, they said, "Let's build a city with a tower that reaches to the sky! We'll use hard bricks and tar instead of stone and mortar. We'll become famous, and we won't be scattered all over the world."

But when the LORD came down to look at the city and the tower, he said, "These people are working together because they all speak the same language. This is just the beginning. Soon they will be able to do anything they want. Come on! Let's go down and confuse them by making them speak different languages—then they won't be able to understand each other."

So the people had to stop building the city, because the LORD confused their language and scattered them all over the earth. That's how the city of Babel got its name.

Based on Genesis 11.1-9

So the people had to stop building the city, because the LORD confused their language and scattered them all over the earth. That's how the city of Babel got its name.

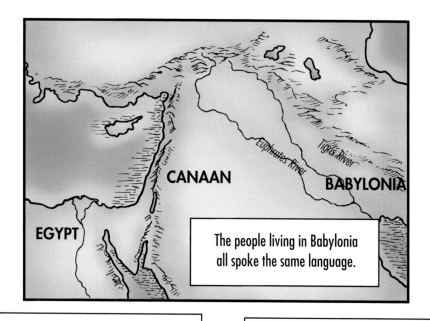

CANAAN

EGYPT

BABYLONIA

Euphrates River

Tigris River

The people living in Babylonia all spoke the same language.

They said to one another, "Let's build a tower that reaches to the sky. We'll make ourselves famous!"

So they made bricks and used them to build a very tall tower.

God saw the tall tower.

The people were too proud.

God confused their language.

They had to stop building.

They scattered all over the earth.

That place was called Babel.

Pack Up and Leave Home!

The LORD said to Abram, "Leave your country, your family, and your relatives and go to the land that I will show you. I will bless you and make your descendants into a great nation. You will become famous and be a blessing to others. I will bless anyone who blesses you, but I will put a curse on anyone who puts a curse on you. Everyone on earth will be blessed because of you."

Abram was seventy-five years old when the LORD told him to leave the city of Haran. He obeyed and left with his wife Sarai, his nephew Lot, and all the possessions and slaves they had gotten while in Haran.

When they came to the land of Canaan, Abram went as far as the sacred tree of Moreh in a place called Shechem. The Canaanites were still living in the land at that time, but the LORD appeared to Abram and promised, "I will give this land to your family forever." Abram then built an altar there for the LORD.

Abram was ninety-nine years old when the Lord appeared to him again. Abram bowed with his face to the ground, and God said: "I promise that you will be the father of many nations. That's why I now change your name from Abram to Abraham. I will give you a lot of descendants, and in the future they will become great nations. Your wife's name will now be Sarah instead of Sarai. I will bless her, and you will have a son by her. She will become the mother of nations."

Based on Genesis 12.1-7; 17.1-16

The LORD said to Abram, "I will bless you and make your descendants into a great nation. You will become famous and be a blessing to others."

God told Abram to leave his home and go to a new land.

Abram and Sarai got ready to leave.

They left for Canaan.

They finally arrived in Canaan.

Abram gave thanks to God.

God promised the new land would belong to Abraham's family forever.

"That's why I now change your name from Abram to Abraham, and I will change your wife's name from Sarai to Sarah."

God Surprises Abraham and Sarah

One hot summer afternoon Abraham was sitting by the entrance to his tent near the sacred trees of Mamre, when the LORD appeared to him. Abraham looked up and saw three men standing nearby. He quickly ran to meet them, bowed with his face to the ground, and said, "Please come to my home where I can serve you. I'll have some water brought, so you can wash your feet, then you can rest under the tree. Let me get you some food to give you strength before you leave. I would be honored to serve you."

"Thank you very much," they answered. "We accept your offer."

Abraham quickly went to his tent and said to Sarah, "Hurry! Get a large sack of flour and make some bread." After saying this, he rushed off to his herd of cattle and picked out one of the best calves, which his servant quickly prepared. He then served his guests some yogurt and milk together with the meat. While they were eating, he stood near them under the trees, and they asked, "Where is your wife Sarah?"

"She is right there in the tent," Abraham answered.

One of the guests was the LORD, and the LORD said, "I'll come back about this time next year, and when I do, Sarah will already have a son." Sarah was behind Abraham, listening at the entrance to the tent. Abraham and Sarah were very old, and Sarah was well past the age of having children. So she laughed and said to herself, "Now that I am worn out and my husband is old, will I really know such happiness?"

The LORD asked Abraham, "Why did Sarah laugh? Does she doubt that she can have a child in her old age? I am the LORD! There is nothing too difficult for me."

The LORD was good to Sarah and kept the promise. Although Abraham was very old, Sarah had a son exactly at the time God had said. Abraham named his son Isaac.

Based on Genesis 18.1-14; 21.1-3

Although Abraham was very old, Sarah had a son exactly at the time God had said.

Three men came to visit Abraham and he invited them in to eat.

Sarah baked bread.

Abraham picked the best calf to cook for the meal.

Abraham talked with the visitors.

Sarah laughed when she heard God promise that she would have a son.

God asked, "Why did Sarah laugh?"

One year later, Isaac was born.

Abraham Makes a Tough Choice

Some years later God decided to test Abraham, so he spoke to him.

Abraham answered, "Here I am, LORD."

The LORD said, "Go get Isaac, your only son, the one you dearly love! Take him to the land of Moriah, and I will show you a mountain where you must sacrifice him to me on the fires of an altar."

So Abraham got up early the next morning and chopped wood for the fire. He put a saddle on his donkey and left with Isaac and two servants for the place where God had told him to go.

Three days later Abraham looked off in the distance and saw the place. He told his servants, "Stay here with the donkey, while my son and I go over there to worship."

As the two of them walked along, Isaac said, "Father, we have the coals and the wood, but where is the lamb for the sacrifice?"

"My son," Abraham answered, "God will provide the lamb."

When they reached the place that God had told him about, Abraham built an altar and placed the wood on it. Next, he tied up his son and put him on the wood. He then took the knife and got ready to kill his son. But the LORD's angel shouted from heaven, "Abraham! Abraham!"

"Here I am!" he answered.

"Don't hurt the boy or harm him in any way!" the angel said. "Now I know that you truly obey God, because you were willing to offer him your only son."

Abraham looked up and saw a ram caught by its horns in the bushes. So he took the ram and sacrificed it in place of his son.

Based on Genesis 22.1-13

The angel said, "Now I know that you truly obey God, because you were willing to offer him your only son."

God told Abraham to sacrifice his son on an altar.

Abraham left with Isaac.

They walked for three days.

"Where is the lamb for the sacrifice?"

Abraham said that God would provide the lamb.

Abraham and Isaac built an altar of stones.

Abraham obeyed God.

God's angel called Abraham's name.

"Don't harm your son."

Abraham sacrificed the ram.

Rebekah Offers Water to a Stranger

One day, Abraham said to his most trusted servant, "Promise me that you won't choose a wife for my son Isaac from the people here in the land of Canaan. Instead, go back to the land where I was born and find a wife for him from among my relatives."

So the servant promised Abraham that he would do everything he had been told to do. Then he set out for the city in northern Syria.

The servant prayed, "You, LORD, are the God my master Abraham worships. Please keep your promise to him and let me find a wife for Isaac today. The young women of the city will soon come to this well for water, and I'll ask one of them for a drink. If she gives me a drink and then offers to get some water for my camels, I'll know she is the one you have chosen." While he was still praying, a beautiful unmarried young woman came by with a water jar on her shoulder. Abraham's servant ran to her and said, "Please let me have a drink of water."

"I'll be glad to," she answered. Then she quickly took the jar from her shoulder and held it while he drank. After he had finished, she said, "Now I'll give your camels all the water they want." She quickly poured out water for them, until his camels had drunk all they wanted. Abraham's servant watched everything Rebekah did, because he wanted to know for certain if this was the woman the LORD had chosen.

The servant had brought along an expensive gold ring and two large gold bracelets. When Rebekah had finished bringing the water, he gave her a ring for her nose and the bracelets for her arms. She told him, "My father is Bethuel. We have a place where you and your men can stay."

Then the servant bowed his head and prayed, "I thank you, LORD God of my master Abraham! You have led me to his relatives and kept your promise to him."

Based on Genesis 24.2-27

"I thank you, LORD God of my master Abraham! You have led me to his relatives and kept your promise to him."

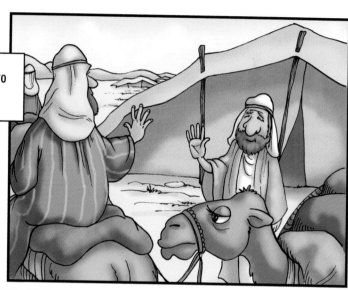

Abraham sent his servant to find a wife for his son.

The servant arrived at a well.

Women came to the well to draw water.

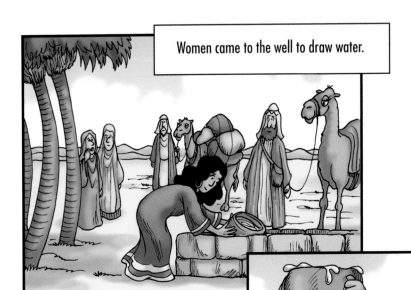

"God, show me which one
will be Isaac's wife."

"If she offers water for
my camels, I'll know
she is the one."

"Would you like some water for your camels?"

The servant knew
Rebekah was the one.

Rebekah invited
them to her home.

Esau and Jacob

Isaac was the son of Abraham, and he was forty years old when he married Rebekah. Almost twenty years later, Rebekah still had no children. So Isaac asked the LORD to let her have a child, and the LORD answered his prayer.

Before Rebekah gave birth, she knew she was going to have twins, because she could feel them inside her, fighting each other. She thought, "Why is this happening to me?" Finally, she asked the LORD why her twins were fighting, and he told her, "Your two sons will become two separate nations. The younger of the two will be stronger, and the older son will be his servant."

When Rebekah gave birth, the first baby was covered with red hair, so he was named Esau. The second baby grabbed on to his brother's heel, so they named him Jacob. Isaac was sixty years old when they were born.

As Jacob and Esau grew older, Esau liked the outdoors and became a good hunter, while Jacob settled down and became a shepherd. Esau would take the meat of wild animals to his father Isaac, and so Isaac loved him more, but Jacob was his mother's favorite son.

One day, Jacob was cooking some stew, when Esau came home hungry and said, "I'm starving to death! Give me some of that red stew right now!"

Jacob replied, "Sell me your rights as the first-born son."

"I'm about to die," Esau answered. "What good will those rights do me?"

But Jacob said, "Promise me your birthrights, here and now!" And that's what Esau did. Jacob then gave Esau some bread and some of the bean stew, and when Esau had finished eating and drinking, he just got up and left, showing how little he thought of his rights as the first-born.

Based on Genesis 25.19-33

*Isaac asked the LORD to let Rebekah have a child,
and the LORD answered his prayer.*

Isaac and Rebekah had no children.

Isaac prayed for a child.

God answered
Isaac's prayer.

Rebekah was
having twins.

They named their sons Esau and Jacob.

Esau became a hunter.

Jacob became a shepherd.

A Ladder to Heaven

Jacob left the town of Beersheba and started out for Haran. At sunset he stopped for the night and went to sleep, resting his head on a large rock. In a dream he saw a ladder that reached from earth to heaven, and God's angels were going up and down on it.

The LORD was standing beside the ladder and said, "I am the LORD God who was worshiped by Abraham and Isaac. I will give to you and your family the land on which you are now sleeping. Wherever you go, I will watch over you, then later I will bring you back to this land. I won't leave you—I will do all I have promised."

Jacob woke up suddenly and thought, "The LORD is in this place, and I didn't even know it." Then Jacob became frightened and said, "This is a fearsome place! It must be the house of God and the ladder to heaven."

When Jacob got up early the next morning, he took the rock that he had used for a pillow and stood it up for a place of worship. Then he poured olive oil on the rock to dedicate it to God, and he named the place Bethel.

Jacob solemnly promised God, "If you go with me and watch over me as I travel, and if you give me food and clothes and bring me safely home again, you will be my God."

Based on Genesis 28.10-21

The LORD told Jacob, "I will give to you and your family the land on which you are now sleeping."

Jacob left for Haran.

Jacob spent the night beside the road.

Jacob dreamed about a ladder up to heaven.

"This must be a holy place!"

Jacob poured olive oil on a rock to thank God.

Jacob promised to serve God always.

Esau Surprises Jacob

Jacob was headed back to his home and thought Esau would still be mad for tricking him out of his birthright. So Jacob sent cattle and sheep as gifts for Esau.

Jacob saw Esau coming with his four hundred men and the gifts. Jacob was afraid, so he had his children walk with their mothers. Jacob walked in front, bowing to the ground seven times as he came near his brother.

But Esau ran toward Jacob and hugged and kissed him. Then the two brothers started crying. When Esau noticed the women and children he asked, "Whose children are these?"

Jacob answered, "These are the ones the LORD has been kind enough to give to me, your servant." All of Jacob's wives and children came and bowed down to Esau.

Esau asked Jacob, "Why did you send me all these cattle and sheep?"

"Master," Jacob answered, "I sent them so that you would be friendly to me."

"But, brother, I already have plenty," Esau replied. "Keep them for yourself."

"No!" Jacob said. "Please accept these gifts as a sign of your friendship for me." Jacob kept insisting until Esau accepted the gifts.

"Let's get ready to travel," Esau said. "I'll go along with you."

But Jacob answered, "Why don't you go on ahead and let me travel along slowly with the children, the herds and the flocks. We can meet up again in Edom."

Esau replied, "Let me leave some of my men with you."

"You don't have to do that," Jacob answered. "I am happy, simply knowing that you are friendly with me." So Esau left for his own country.

Based on Genesis 33.1-16

*Jacob said to Esau, "Please accept these gifts
as a sign of your friendship for me."*

A long time ago, Jacob tricked his brother Esau.

Jacob was now afraid
to see him again.

But Esau had forgiven Jacob.

"Who are these children?"

"God has blessed me with this large family."

"Why did you send me these animals?"

"So you would forgive me."

A Coat of Love and Hate

Jacob lived in the land of Canaan, where his father Isaac had lived, and this is the story of his family.

When Jacob's son Joseph was seventeen years old, he took care of the sheep with his brothers, the sons of Bilhah and Zilpah. But he was always telling his father all sorts of bad things about his brothers.

Jacob loved Joseph more than he did any of his other sons, because Joseph was born after Jacob was very old. Jacob had given Joseph a fancy coat to show that he was his favorite son, and so Joseph's brothers hated him and would not be friendly to him.

One day when Joseph's brothers had taken the sheep to a pasture near Shechem, his father Jacob said to him, "I want you to go to your brothers. They are with the sheep near Shechem."

"Yes, sir," Joseph answered.

His father said, "Go and find out how your brothers and the sheep are doing. Then come back and let me know." So he sent him from Hebron Valley.

Joseph found his brothers in Dothan. But before he got there, they saw him coming and made plans to kill him. They said to one another, "Look, here comes Joseph. Let's kill him and throw him into a pit and say that some wild animal ate him."

Reuben heard this and tried to protect Joseph from them. "Let's not kill him," he said. "Don't murder him or even harm him. Just throw him into a dry well out here in the desert." Reuben planned to rescue Joseph later and take him back to his father.

When Joseph came to his brothers, they pulled off his fancy coat and threw him into a dry well.

As Joseph's brothers sat down to eat, they looked up and saw a caravan of traders coming from Gilead. Their camels were loaded with all kinds of spices that they were taking to Egypt. So Judah said, "What will we gain if we kill our brother and hide his body? Let's sell him to the traders and not harm him. After all, he is our brother." And the others agreed.

When the traders came by, Joseph's brothers took him out of the well, and for twenty pieces of silver they sold him to the traders who took him to Egypt.

When Reuben returned to the well and did not find Joseph there, he tore his clothes in sorrow. Then he went back to his brothers and said, "The boy is gone! What am I going to do?"

Joseph's brothers killed a goat and dipped Joseph's fancy coat in its blood. After this, they took the coat to their father and said, "We found this! Look at it carefully and see if it belongs to your son."

Jacob knew it was Joseph's coat and said, "It's my son's coat! Joseph has been torn to pieces and eaten by some wild animal."

Jacob mourned for Joseph a long time, and to show his sorrow he tore his clothes and wore sackcloth. All of Jacob's children came to comfort him, but he refused to be comforted.

Based on Genesis 37.1-4, 12-35

Jacob loved Joseph more than he did any of his other sons.

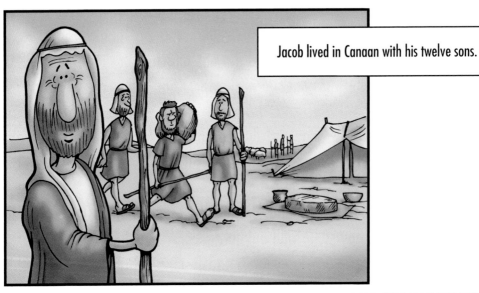

Jacob lived in Canaan with his twelve sons.

Jacob loved his son Joseph the most and gave him a special coat.

Joseph's brothers saw
the coat and got angry.

Jacob sent Joseph to
be with his brothers.

Joseph's brothers were
angry when they saw
him coming.

They ripped off
Joseph's coat and
threw him into
the well.

The brothers sold
Joseph as a
slave to traders
going to Egypt.

"We will tell our
father an animal
killed Joseph."

They showed Jacob the coat.

Jacob thought his son was dead.

A Leader in a Foreign Land

One day, the king of Egypt dreamed he was standing beside the Nile River. Suddenly, seven fat, healthy cows came up from the river and started eating grass along the bank. Then seven ugly, skinny cows came up out of the river and ate the fat, healthy cows. When this happened, the king woke up.

The king went back to sleep and had another dream. This time seven full heads of grain were growing on a single stalk. Later, seven other heads of grain appeared, but they were thin and scorched by the east wind. The thin heads of grain swallowed the seven full heads. Again the king woke up, and it had only been a dream.

The next morning the king was upset. So he called in his magicians and wise men and told them what he had dreamed. None of them could tell him what the dreams meant.

The king sent for Joseph, who was quickly brought out of jail. He shaved, changed his clothes, and went to the king.

The king said to him, "I had a dream, yet no one can explain what it means. I am told that you can interpret dreams."

"Your Majesty," Joseph answered, "I can't do it myself, but God can give a meaning to your dreams." So the king told Joseph his dreams.

Joseph replied, "Both of your dreams mean the same thing, and in them God has shown what he is going to do. For seven years Egypt will have more than enough grain, but that will be followed by seven years when there won't be enough. The good years of plenty will be forgotten, and everywhere in Egypt people will be starving. The famine will be so bad that no one will remember that once there had been plenty. God has given you two dreams to let you know that he has definitely decided to do this and that he will do it soon.

"Your Majesty, you should find someone who is wise and will know what to do, so that you can put him in charge of all Egypt. Then appoint some other officials to collect one-fifth of every crop harvested in Egypt during the seven years when there is plenty. Give them the power to collect the grain during those good years and to store it in your cities. It can be stored until it is needed during the seven years when there won't be enough grain in Egypt. This will keep the country from being destroyed because of the lack of food."

The king and his officials liked this plan. So the king said to them, "No one could possibly handle this better than Joseph, since the Spirit of God is with him."

Joseph was thirty when the king made him governor, and he went everywhere for the king. For seven years there were big harvests of grain. Joseph collected and stored up the extra grain in the cities of Egypt near the fields where it was harvested. In fact, there was so much grain that they stopped keeping record, because it was like counting the grains of sand along the beach.

Egypt's seven years of plenty came to an end, and the seven years of famine began, just as Joseph had said. There was not enough food in other countries, but all over Egypt there was plenty. When the famine finally struck Egypt, the people asked the king for food, but he said, "Go to Joseph and do what he tells you to do."

The famine became bad everywhere in Egypt, so Joseph opened the store-houses and sold the grain to the Egyptians. People from all over the world came to Egypt, because the famine was severe in their countries.

Based on Genesis 41.1-57

The king of Egypt said to his officials, "No one could possibly handle this plan better than Joseph, since the Spirit of God is with him."

The king of Egypt had two bad dreams.

The king asked what the dreams meant.

"I saw seven skinny cows eat seven fat cows."

"I saw seven skinny heads of grain eat seven fat ones."

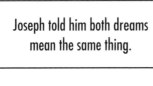

Joseph told him both dreams mean the same thing.

Egypt will have seven years of good crops followed by seven years of no crops.

The king made Joseph in charge of the grain.

Egypt had seven years of famine.

Joseph made sure everyone had food.

Joseph even gave grain to people from other countries.

Jacob Gets a New Home

When Jacob found out that there was grain in Egypt, he said to his sons, "Why are you just sitting here, staring at one another? I have heard there is grain in Egypt. Now go down and buy some, so we won't starve to death." Ten of Jacob's sons went to Egypt to buy grain.

When they stood before Joseph to ask for food, he did not tell them who he was because of the way they had treated him. Only later did he forgive them and say, "I am your brother Joseph." The king then told Joseph to send his brothers back to Canaan and bring their father Jacob and their entire family to live in Egypt.

So Joseph's brothers left Egypt, and when they arrived in Canaan, they told their father that Joseph was still alive and was the ruler of Egypt. But their father was so surprised that he could not believe them. Then they told him everything Joseph had said. When he saw the wagons Joseph had sent, he felt much better and said, "Now I can believe you! My son Joseph must really be alive, and I will get to see him before I die."

Jacob packed up everything he owned and left for Egypt. On the way he stopped near the town of Beersheba and offered sacrifices to the God his father Isaac had worshiped. That night, God spoke to him and said, "Jacob! Jacob!"

"Here I am," Jacob answered.

God said, "I am God, the same God your father worshiped. Don't be afraid to go to Egypt. I will give you so many descendants that one day they will become a nation. I will go with you to Egypt, and later I will bring your descendants back here. Your son Joseph will be at your side when you die."

Jacob and his family set out from Beersheba and headed for Egypt. His sons put him in the wagon that the king had sent for him, and they put their small children and their wives in the other wagons. Jacob's whole family went to Egypt, including his sons, his grandsons, his daughters, and his granddaughters. They took along their animals and everything else they owned.

When they arrived in Egypt, Jacob and his family settled in the fertile land of Goshen. Jacob and his family lived there and the king of Egypt treated them like his own family. Just before Jacob died, he gathered his sons around him and told them to bury him in Canaan, the land God had promised his grandfather Abraham.

Based on Genesis 42–50

God said to Jacob, "I am God, the same God your father worshiped. Don't be afraid to go to Egypt. I will give you so many descendants that one day they will become a nation."

Jacob sent his sons to Egypt to buy food.

They did not recognize their brother Joseph.

He told them to bring their father to Egypt.

Jacob moved his family to Egypt.

Along the way, Jacob built an altar to thank God.

God told Jacob that one day his descendants would return to Canaan.

Jacob and Joseph were together again!

Jacob lived in Egypt the rest of his life.

A Safe Place To Hide a Baby

Many years after Joseph's death, the new king of Egypt knew nothing about the good things he had done for Egypt. Because the king believed too many Hebrews (Jacob's descendants) lived in Egypt, he made them slaves but the number of Hebrews kept increasing. So the king commanded that every Hebrew baby boy born be thrown into the Nile River.

A man from the Levi tribe married a woman from the same tribe, and she later had a baby boy. He was a beautiful child, and she kept him inside for three months, but when she could no longer keep him hidden, she made a basket out of reeds and covered it with tar. She put him in the basket and placed it in the tall grass along the edge of the Nile River. The baby's older sister stood off at a distance to see what would happen to him.

About that time one of the king's daughters came down to take a bath in the river, while her servant women walked along the river bank. She saw the basket in the tall grass and sent one of the young women to pull it out of the water. When the king's daughter opened the basket, she saw the baby and felt sorry for him because he was crying. She said, "This must be one of the Hebrew babies."

At once the baby's older sister came up and asked, "Do you want me to get a Hebrew woman to take care of the baby for you?"

"Yes," the king's daughter answered.

So the girl brought the baby's mother, and the king's daughter told her, "Take care of this child, and I will pay you."

The baby's mother carried him home and took care of him. And when he was old enough, she took him to the king's daughter, who adopted him. She named him Moses because she said, "I pulled him out of the water."

Based on Exodus 2.1-10

When Moses was old enough, his mother took him to the king's daughter, who adopted him. The king's daughter named him Moses because she said, "I pulled him out of the water."

The king of Egypt had every Hebrew baby boy thrown into the Nile River.

A Hebrew man and his wife had a baby boy.

The mother and sister made a basket to hide him.

The mother laid her baby in the basket.

His older sister watched what would happen.

The king's daughter saw the basket.

She saw the baby and felt sorry for him.

The baby's sister offered to get a Hebrew woman to take care of him.

She brought the baby's mother.

The king's daughter adopted him and named him Moses.

A Burning Bush That Talks

One day, Moses was taking care of the sheep and decided to lead them to Sinai, the holy mountain. There an angel of the LORD appeared to Moses from a burning bush. Moses saw that the bush was on fire, but not burning up. "This is strange!" he said. "I'll go over and see why the bush isn't burning up."

When the LORD saw Moses coming near the bush, he called him by name, and Moses answered, "Here I am."

God replied, "Don't come any closer. Take off your sandals—the ground where you are standing is holy. I am the God who was worshiped by your ancestors Abraham, Isaac, and Jacob."

Moses was afraid to look at God, and so he hid his face. The LORD said, "I have seen how my people are suffering as slaves in Egypt, and I have heard them beg for my help because of the way they are being mistreated. I feel sorry for them, and I have come down to rescue them from the Egyptians. I will bring my people out of Egypt into a country where there is good land, rich with milk and honey. Now go to the king! I am sending you to lead my people out of his country."

But Moses said, "Who am I to go to the king and lead your people out of Egypt?"

God replied, "I will be with you. And you will know that I am the one who sent you, when you worship me on this mountain after you have led my people out of Egypt."

Moses answered, "I will tell the people of Israel that the God their ancestors worshiped has sent me to them. But what should I say, if they ask me your name?"

God said to Moses, "I am the eternal God. So tell them that the LORD, whose name is 'I Am,' has sent you. This is my name forever, and it is the name that people must use from now on."

Based on Exodus 3.1-15

God said to Moses, "I am the eternal God. So tell them that the LORD, whose name is 'I Am,' has sent you. This is my name forever, and it is the name that people must use from now on."

While Moses was tending sheep, he saw a burning bush.

Moses thought, "Why is it not burning up?"

"I am your God. Take off your sandals because this place is holy."

God replied,
"I will be with you."

"What should I say if they ask me your name?"

"I am the eternal God whose name is I AM."

Moses Is Not Alone

Moses and his brother Aaron went to the king of Egypt and told him to let the Hebrew people go free. These words made the king angry so he made the people work even harder

Moses prayed, "Our LORD, why have you brought so much trouble on your people? Is that why you sent me here? Ever since you told me to speak to the king, he has caused nothing but trouble for these people. And you haven't done a thing to help."

The LORD God told Moses:

Soon you will see what I will do to the king. Because of my mighty power, he will let my people go, and he will even chase them out of his country.

My name is the LORD. But when I appeared to Abraham, Isaac, and Jacob, I came as God All-Powerful and did not use my name. I made an agreement and promised them the land of Canaan, where they were living as foreigners. Now I have seen how the people of Israel are suffering because of the Egyptians, and I will keep my promise.

Here is my message for Israel: "I am the LORD! And with my mighty power I will punish the Egyptians and free you from slavery. I will accept you as my people, and I will be your God. Then you will know that I was the one who rescued you from the Egyptians. I will bring you into the land that I solemnly promised Abraham, Isaac, and Jacob, and it will be yours. I am the LORD!"

When Moses told this to the Israelites, they were too discouraged and mistreated to believe him.

Then the LORD told Moses to demand that the king of Egypt let the Israelites leave. But Moses replied, "I'm not a powerful speaker. If the Israelites won't listen to me, why should the king of Egypt?" But the LORD sent Aaron and Moses with a message for the Israelites and for the king; he also ordered Aaron and Moses to free the people from Egypt.

Based on Exodus 5.22–6.13

"Here is my message for Israel: 'I am the LORD! And with my mighty power I will punish the Egyptians and free you from slavery.'"

"LORD, why have you brought so much trouble on your people?"

God answered, "Tell my people I will lead them out of Egypt."

"They will inherit the land of Canaan."

The people refused to believe Moses.

God said, "Tell the king to let my people go."

"If the Israelites won't listen to me, why should the king?"

Moses' brother Aaron went with him to speak to the king.

Time To Leave

The LORD spoke to Moses in the land of Egypt and said, "I am the LORD. Tell the king of Egypt everything I say to you." Moses and Aaron obeyed the LORD and spoke to the king.

But just as the LORD had said, the king stubbornly refused to listen to them. So the LORD made terrible things (called plagues) happen to the people of Egypt. The LORD caused the Nile River to turn into blood, then sent frogs, gnats, and flies to cover the land. The LORD sent a disease that killed cattle and horses, sores that broke out on people, locusts that ate the crops, and darkness that covered the entire land. None of these terrible things happened to the Hebrews. Still the king of Egypt refused to let the Hebrews go free.

Then, the LORD said to Moses, "I am going to punish the king of Egypt and his people one more time. Then the king will gladly let you leave his land, so that I will stop punishing the Egyptians. He will even chase you out."

Moses went to the king and said, "I have come to let you know what the LORD is going to do. About midnight he will go through the land of Egypt and wherever he goes, the first-born son in every family will die. Even the first-born cattle will die. Everywhere in Egypt there will be a loud crying. But there won't be any need for the Israelites to cry. Things will be so quiet that not even a dog will be heard barking. Then you Egyptians will know that the LORD is good to the Israelites, even while he punishes you. Your leaders will come and bow down, begging me to take my people and leave your country. Then we will leave." Moses was very angry; he turned and left the king.

At midnight the LORD killed the first-born son of every Egyptian family, from the son of the king to the son of every prisoner in jail. He also killed the first-born male of every animal that belonged to the Egyptians.

That night the king, his officials, and everyone else in Egypt got up and started crying bitterly. In every Egyptian home, someone was dead.

During the night the king sent for Moses and Aaron and told them, "Get your people out of my country and leave us alone! Go and worship the LORD, as you have asked. Take your sheep, goats, and cattle, and get out. But ask your God to be kind to me."

The Egyptians did everything they could to get the Israelites to leave their country fast. They said, "Please hurry and leave. If you don't, we will all be dead." So the Israelites quickly made some bread dough and put it in pans. But they did not mix any yeast in the dough to make it rise. They wrapped cloth around the pans and carried them on their shoulders. The LORD's people left Egypt exactly four hundred thirty years after they had arrived.

The LORD led them around through the desert and toward the Red Sea.

Based on Exodus 6.28–13.18

The LORD said to Moses, "I am going to punish the king of Egypt and his people one more time. Then the king will gladly let you leave his land, so that I will stop punishing the Egyptians."

Moses and Aaron told the king of Egypt to let the Hebrew people free, but he refused.

God made terrible things happen to the people of Egypt. The river turned to blood.

91

God sent darkness.

The king still would not let the people go free.

God said every first-born Egyptian son would die.

Even the king's son died.

The Hebrews were safe.

The king finally let the Hebrews leave Egypt.

The Hebrews packed up their belongings.

God led the Hebrews out of Egypt.

Miracle at the Sea

When the king of Egypt heard that the Israelites had finally left, he and his officials changed their minds and said, "Look what we have done! We let them get away, and they will no longer be our slaves."

The king got his war chariot and army ready. He commanded his officers in charge of his six hundred best chariots and all his other chariots to start after the Israelites. The LORD made the king so stubborn that he went after them, even though the Israelites proudly went on their way. But the king's horses and chariots and soldiers caught up with them while they were camping by the Red Sea.

When the Israelites saw the king coming with his army, they were frightened and begged the LORD for help. They also complained to Moses, "Wasn't there enough room in Egypt to bury us? Is that why you brought us out here to die in the desert? Why did you bring us out of Egypt anyway? While we were there, didn't we tell you to leave us alone? We had rather be slaves in Egypt than die in this desert!"

But Moses answered, "Don't be afraid! Be brave, and you will see the LORD save you today. These Egyptians will never bother you again. The LORD will fight for you, and you won't have to do a thing."

The LORD said to Moses, "Tell the Israelites to move forward. Then hold your walking stick over the sea. The water will open up and make a road where they can walk through on dry ground. I will make the Egyptians so stubborn that they will go after you. Then I will be praised because of what happens to the king and his chariots and cavalry. The Egyptians will know for sure that I am the LORD."

All this time God's angel had gone ahead of Israel's army, but now he moved behind them. A large cloud had also gone ahead of them, but now it moved between the Egyptians and the Israelites. The cloud gave light to the Israelites, but made it dark for the Egyptians, and during the night they could not come any closer.

Moses stretched his arm over the sea, and the LORD sent a strong east wind that blew all night until there was dry land where the water had been. The sea opened up, and the Israelites walked through on dry land with a wall of water on each side.

The Egyptian chariots and cavalry went after them. But before daylight the LORD looked down at the Egyptian army from the fiery cloud and made them panic. Their chariot wheels got stuck, and it was hard for them to move. So the Egyptians said to one another, "Let's leave these people alone! The LORD is on their side and is fighting against us."

The LORD told Moses, "Stretch your arm toward the sea the water will cover the Egyptians and their cavalry and chariots." Moses stretched out his arm, and at daybreak the water rushed toward the Egyptians. They tried to run away, but the LORD drowned them in the sea. The water came and covered the chariots, the cavalry, and the whole Egyptian army that had followed the Israelites into the sea. Not one of them was left alive.

On that day, the Israelites knew that the LORD had saved them. Because of the mighty power he had used against the Egyptians, the Israelites worshiped him and trusted him and his servant Moses.

Based on Exodus 14.5-31

Because of the mighty power the LORD had used against the Egyptians, the Israelites worshiped him and trusted him and his servant Moses.

The king of Egypt changed his mind.

The king and his soldiers chased after the Israelites.

The Israelites were afraid.

"Don't be afraid—God will save you."

The waves crashed
over the soldiers.

God had rescued
the Israelites!

Food from Heaven

After the Israelites had escaped from Egypt, they started through the western edge of the Sinai Desert in the direction of Mount Sinai. There in the desert they started complaining to Moses and Aaron, "We wish the LORD had killed us in Egypt. When we lived there, we could at least sit down and eat all the bread and meat we wanted. But you have brought us out here into this desert, where we are going to starve."

The LORD said to Moses, "I have heard my people complain. Now tell them that each evening they will have meat and each morning they will have more than enough bread. Then they will know that I am the LORD their God."

That evening a lot of quails came and landed everywhere in the camp, and the next morning dew covered the ground. After the dew had gone, the desert was covered with thin flakes that looked like frost. The people had never seen anything like this, and they started asking each other, "What is it?"

Moses answered, "This is the bread that the LORD has given you to eat."

The Israelites called the bread manna. It looked like tiny white seeds and tasted like wafers made with honey.

Based on Exodus 16.1-15, 31

The LORD said to Moses, "I have heard my people complain. Now tell them that each evening they will have meat and each morning they will have more than enough bread."

The Israelites traveled toward Mount Sinai.

"We have no food."

"God will send you meat and bread every day."

God sent lots of quail.

103

The Rock Gushes with Water

The Israelites left the desert and moved from one place to another each time the LORD directed them. While they were camped at Rephidim, there was no water for them to drink.

The people started complaining to Moses, "Give us some water!"

Moses replied, "Why are you complaining to me and trying to put the LORD to the test?"

But the people were thirsty and kept on complaining, "Moses, did you bring us out of Egypt just to let us and our families and our animals die of thirst?"

Then Moses prayed to the LORD, "What am I going to do with these people? They are about to stone me to death!"

The LORD answered, "Take some of the leaders with you and go ahead of the rest of the people. Also take along the walking stick you used to strike the Nile River, and when you get to the rock at Mount Sinai, I will be there with you. Strike the rock with the stick, and water will pour out for the people to drink." Moses did this while the leaders watched.

Based on Exodus 17.1-6

*The LORD said to Moses, "Strike the rock with the stick,
and water will pour out for the people to drink."*

The Israelites camped
in the desert.

"We have no water!"

Moses asked God for water.

God sent Moses to a special rock at Mount Sinai.

107

Top Ten Ways To Obey God

Two months after the Israelites left Egypt, they arrived at the desert near Mount Sinai, where they set up camp at the foot of the mountain. Moses went up the mountain to meet with the LORD God.

God said to the people of Israel:

I am the LORD your God, the one who brought you out of Egypt where you were slaves.

Do not worship any god except me.

Do not make idols that look like anything in the sky or on earth or in the ocean under the earth. Don't bow down and worship idols.

Do not misuse my name. I am the LORD your God, and I will punish anyone who misuses my name.

Remember that the Sabbath Day belongs to me. You have six days when you can do your work, but the seventh day of each week belongs to me, your God.

Respect your father and your mother, and you will live a long time in the land I am giving you.

Do not murder.

Be faithful in marriage.

Do not steal.

Do not tell lies about others.

Do not want anything that belongs to someone else. Don't want anyone's house, wife or husband, slaves, oxen, donkeys or anything else.

Based on Exodus 19.1-3; 20.1-17

"I am the LORD your God, the one who brought you out of Egypt where you were slaves."

God gave Moses and the people the Ten Commandments.

Treat Everyone with Respect

The LORD said:

If any of your people become poor and unable to support themselves, you must help them, just as you are supposed to help foreigners who live among you. Don't take advantage of them by charging any kind of interest or selling them food for profit. Instead, honor me by letting them stay where they now live. Remember I am the LORD your God! I rescued you from Egypt and gave you the land of Canaan, so that I would be your God.

Suppose some of your people become so poor that they have to sell themselves and become your slaves. Then you must treat them as servants, rather than as slaves. And in the Year of Celebration they are to be set free, so they and their children may return home to their families and property. I brought them out of Egypt to be my servants, not to be sold as slaves. So obey me, and don't be cruel to the poor.

Based on Leviticus 25.35-43

The LORD said, "Don't be cruel to the poor."

Help people who are unable to work.

Do not make money by selling food to the poor.

113

Do not throw poor people out of their homes.

Be kind to people who work for you.

115

Exploring a New Land

The LORD said to Moses, "Choose a leader from each tribe and send them into Canaan to explore the land I am giving you."

So Moses sent twelve leaders from Israel's camp with orders to explore the land of Canaan.

But before Moses sent them, he said, "Be sure to remember how many people live there, how strong they are and if they live in open towns or walled cities. See if the land is good for growing crops and find out what kinds of trees grow there. It's time for grapes to ripen, so try to bring back some of the fruit that grows there."

After exploring the land forty days, the twelve men returned and told Moses, Aaron, and the people what they had seen.

They showed them the fruit and said, "Look at this fruit! The land we explored is rich with milk and honey. But the people who live there are strong, and their cities are large and walled."

Caleb, one of the twelve men, calmed down the crowd and said, "Let's go and take the land. I know we can do it!" But the other men replied, "Those people are much too strong for us."

Then the other men started spreading rumors and saying, "We won't be able to grow anything in that soil. And the people are like giants. They were so big that we felt as small as grasshoppers."

Based on Numbers 13.1-32

Caleb calmed down the crowd and said,
"Let's go and take the land. I know we can do it!"

Moses sent twelve men to explore the new land.

They saw a land with lots of fruit and crops.

117

But they were afraid of the people.

The men brought back fruit and grain.

Ten of them did not want to go back to the land.

Caleb was not afraid...

but the other men told lies about the new land and its people.

Remember These Words!

Moses said to Israel:

The LORD told me to give you these laws and teachings, so you can obey them in the land he is giving you. Soon you will cross the Jordan River and take that land. And if you and your descendants want to live a long time, you must always worship the LORD and obey his laws. Pay attention, Israel! Our ancestors worshiped the LORD, and he promised to give us this land that is rich with milk and honey. Be careful to obey him, and you will become a successful and powerful nation.

Listen, Israel! The LORD our God is the only true God! So love the LORD your God with all your heart, soul, and strength. Memorize his laws and tell them to your children over and over again. Talk about them all the time, whether you're at home or walking along the road or going to bed at night, or getting up in the morning. Write down copies and tie them to your wrists and foreheads to help you obey them. Write these laws on the door frames of your homes and on your town gates.

Based on Deuteronomy 6.1-9

Love the LORD your God with all your heart, soul, and strength.

"Soon you will cross the Jordan River."

"Obey all the commandments God has given us."

"Love God completely."

"Memorize and teach God's commandments."

122

A New Home Across the River

Moses spoke to the nation of Israel, "I am a hundred twenty years old, and I am no longer able to be your leader. God has promised that Joshua will lead you across the Jordan River. Be brave and strong! The LORD your God will always be at your side and will never abandon you."

Joshua and the Israelites packed up their belongings and went to the Jordan River and camped. Two days later their leaders went through the camp, shouting, "When you see some of the priests carrying the sacred chest, you'll know it is time to cross to the other side. You've never been there before, and you won't know the way, unless you follow the chest."

Joshua told the people, "Make yourselves acceptable to worship the LORD, because he is going to do some amazing things for us."

Then Joshua turned to the priests and said, "Take the chest and cross the Jordan River ahead of us." So the priests picked up the chest by its carrying poles and went on ahead.

The LORD told Joshua, "Beginning today I will show the people that you are their leader, and they will know that I am helping you as I helped Moses."

The Israelites packed up and left camp. The priests carrying the chest walked in front, until they came to the Jordan River. As soon as the feet of the priests touched the water, the river stopped flowing, and the water started piling up. The priests stood in the middle of the dry riverbed near Jericho while everyone else crossed over.

Then the priests carried the chest past the highest place that the floodwaters of the Jordan had reached, and the river flooded its banks again.

That's how the LORD showed the Israelites that Joshua was their leader. For the rest of Joshua's life, they respected him as they had respected Moses.

Based on Deuteronomy 31.1-6; Joshua 3.1-17; 4.1-18

The LORD told Joshua, "Beginning today I will show the people that you are their leader, and they will know that I am helping you as I helped Moses."

Moses announces Joshua is the new leader.

The Israelites camped by the Jordan River.

"God will do amazing things for us."

The priests carried the sacred chest.

The water parted.

126

The water started flowing again.

The people knew Joshua was their leader.

Watch for Falling Walls!

The LORD said to Joshua, "With my help, you and your army will defeat the king of Jericho and his army, and you will capture the town. Here is how to do it: March slowly around Jericho once a day for six days. Take along the sacred chest and have seven priests walk in front of it, carrying trumpets.

"But on the seventh day, march slowly around the town seven times while the priests blow their trumpets. Then the priests will blast on their trumpets, and everyone else will shout. The wall will fall down, and your soldiers can go straight in from every side."

Joshua and everyone else started marching around Jericho. One group of soldiers was in front, followed by the seven priests with trumpets and the priests who carried the chest. The seven priests blew their trumpets while everyone marched slowly around Jericho and back to camp. They did this once a day for six days.

On the seventh day, the army got up at daybreak. They marched slowly around Jericho the same as they had done for the past six days, except on this day they went around seven times. Then the priests blew the trumpets, and Joshua yelled, "Get ready to shout! The LORD will let you capture this town."

The priests blew their trumpets again, and the soldiers shouted as loud as they could. The walls of Jericho fell flat.

Based on Joshua 6.1-20

The priests blew their trumpets again, and the soldiers shouted as loud as they could. The walls of Jericho fell flat.

God said, "Joshua, I will help you capture Jericho."

The priests carried the sacred chest.

The Israelites marched around Jericho.

On the seventh day, they blew horns and shouted.

The walls of Jericho fell flat!

Ruth Refuses To Leave

Before Israel was ruled by kings, a man named Elimelech, his wife Naomi and their two sons lived in the town of Bethlehem. But when their crops failed, they moved to the country of Moab. And while they were there, Elimelech died, leaving Naomi with only her two sons.

Later, Naomi's sons married Moabite women. One was named Orpah and the other Ruth. About ten years later, the two sons also died. Now Naomi had no husband or sons.

When Naomi heard that the LORD had given his people a good harvest, she and her two daughters-in-law got ready to leave Moab and go to Judah. As they were on their way there, Naomi said to them, "Don't you want to go back home to your own mothers? I pray that the Lord will give each of you another husband and a home of your own."

Naomi kissed them. They cried and said, "We want to go with you and live among your people."

But she replied, "My daughters, why don't you return home?"

They cried again. Orpah kissed her mother-in-law good-by, but Ruth held on to her. Naomi then said to Ruth, "Look, your sister-in-law is going back to her people and to her gods! Why don't you go with her?"

Ruth answered, "Please don't tell me to leave you and return home! I will go where you go, I will live where you live; your people will be my people, your God will be my God."

When Naomi saw that Ruth had made up her mind to go with her, she stopped urging her to go back. They reached Bethlehem, and the whole town was excited to see them.

Based on Ruth 1.1-19

132

*I will go where you go, I will live where you live;
your people will be my people, your God will be my God.*

Naomi lived with her husband and sons in Bethlehem.

When the crops failed, Naomi and her family moved to Moab.

Naomi's sons married Ruth and Orpah.

Naomi's husband died.

Ten years later her sons died.

Naomi told her daughters-in-law to return home.

Ruth refused to leave.

Naomi and Ruth returned to Bethlehem.

Boaz Meets Ruth

One day, after returning to Bethlehem, Ruth went out to pick up grain in a field owned by Boaz, a relative of Naomi's husband. So Ruth worked in the fields until the barley and wheat were harvested.

Some time later, Naomi said to Ruth: "It's time I found you a husband, who will give you a home and take care of you. You have been picking up grain alongside the women who work for Boaz. Tonight he will be threshing the grain. Now take a bath and put on some perfume, then dress in your best clothes. Watch where he goes to spend the night. Then when he is asleep, lie down at his feet. He will tell you what to do."

Ruth answered, "I'll do whatever you say." She went out to the place where Boaz was working and did what Naomi had told her. When Boaz fell asleep next to a pile of grain, Ruth slipped over quietly. She lay down near his feet.

In the middle of the night, Boaz suddenly woke up and was shocked to see a woman lying at his feet. "Who are you?" he asked.

"Sir, I am Ruth," she answered, "and you are the relative who is supposed to take care of me."

Boaz replied, "The Lord bless you! You could have looked for a younger man, either rich or poor, but you didn't. Don't worry; I'll do what you have asked." Boaz then met with Ruth's family and made arrangements to marry her.

Boaz married Ruth, and the Lord blessed her with a son. The neighborhood women named him Obed. When Obed grew up he had a son named Jesse, who later became the father of King David.

Based on Ruth 2–4

Boaz married Ruth, and the LORD *blessed her with a son.*

"I need to work to get our food."

Boaz let Ruth gather grain in his fields.

At night, Ruth brought the grain home.

"It's time I found you a new husband."

"Stay near Boaz tonight—
maybe he will agree to marry you."

Ruth slept near Boaz.

Boaz woke up and found Ruth next to him.

"I will take care of you."

So Boaz married Ruth...

and later had a baby boy.

Hannah Prays for a Son

Elkanah and his wife Hannah had no children. Once a year, they went to the town of Shiloh to worship God and offer sacrifices.

One year, after offering their sacrifices, Hannah was very sad. She cried as she prayed to the LORD, "I am your servant and I am so miserable! Please let me have a son. I will give him to you for as long as he lives."

Eli the priest overheard Hannah praying and said, "Go home now and stop worrying. I'm sure the God of Israel will answer your prayers." So she and her husband returned home. Some time later the LORD blessed Hannah with a son. She named him Samuel.

When Samuel was old enough, his parents brought him with them to offer their yearly sacrifice. Afterwards, Hannah took Samuel to Eli the priest and said, "Sir, a few years ago I asked the LORD to give me a child. Here he is! The LORD gave me just what I asked for. Now I am giving him to the LORD, and he will be the LORD's servant for as long as he lives."

Elkanah and Hannah went back home, but Samuel stayed to help Eli serve the LORD.

Samuel served the LORD and wore a special linen garment and the clothes his mother made for him. Every year she would bring him new clothes when she and her husband came to offer sacrifices at Shiloh.

Based on 1 Samuel 1.10-28; 2.11-19

"I am giving Samuel to the LORD, and he will be the LORD's servant for as long as he lives."

Elkanah and Hannah went to worship God.

But Hannah was very sad because she had no children.

Hannah asked God for a son.

She promised that her son would serve God.

Eli said, "God will answer your prayers."

Hannah named her son Samuel.

Samuel went with his parents to worship God.

Hannah kept her promise and gave Samuel to God as a servant.

Samuel grew up helping Eli serve God.

Samuel Hears a Voice in the Night

Samuel served the LORD by helping Eli the priest. One night, while Samuel was sleeping, the LORD called out his name. "Here I am!" Samuel answered. Then he ran to Eli and said, "What do you want?"

"I didn't call you," Eli answered. "Go back to bed." Samuel went back.

Again the LORD called out Samuel's name. Samuel got up and went to Eli. But each time Eli told him, "Son, I didn't call you. Go back to sleep."

When the LORD called out Samuel's name for the third time, he went to Eli again and said, "Here I am. What do you want?"

Eli finally realized that it was the LORD who was speaking to Samuel. So he said, "Go back and lie down! If someone speaks to you again, answer, 'I'm listening, LORD. What do you want me to do?'" Once again Samuel went back and laid down.

The LORD then stood beside Samuel and called, "Samuel! Samuel!"

"I'm listening," Samuel answered. "What do you want me to do?"

The LORD said, "I will punish Eli and his family, for cheating people out of their sacrifices to me. Eli knew that his sons refused to respect me and he let them get away with it."

The next morning, Samuel was afraid to tell Eli what the LORD had said. But Eli told him, "Samuel, my boy, come here! What did God say to you? Tell me everything."

Samuel told Eli everything. Then Eli said, "The LORD will do what's right."

As Samuel grew up, the LORD helped him and made everything Samuel said come true. Everyone knew that he was truly the LORD's prophet.

Based on 1 Samuel 3.1-20

"I'm listening," Samuel answered. "What do you want me to do?"

Samuel helped Eli the priest.

One night, Samuel heard a voice call out his name.

"Sir, what do you want?"

"Samuel, I didn't call you."

146

Long Live King Saul!

One day, Israel's leaders came to Samuel the prophet and said, "You are an old man. You set a good example as our leader, but now we want a king to be our leader, just like all the other nations. Choose one for us!"

So Samuel the prophet sent messengers to tell the Israelites to come and meet the LORD. When everyone had arrived, Samuel said, "The LORD God of Israel told me to remind you that he had rescued you from the Egyptians and from your troubles and hard times. Now you have asked for a king. Each tribe and clan must come near the place of worship so the LORD can choose a king."

Samuel brought each tribe, one after the other, to the altar, and the LORD chose the Benjamin tribe. Next, Samuel brought each clan of Benjamin there, and the LORD chose the Matri clan. Finally, Saul was chosen. But when they looked for him, he was nowhere to be found.

The people prayed, "Our LORD, is Saul here?"

"Yes," the LORD answered, "he is hiding behind the baggage."

The people ran and got Saul and brought him into the middle of the crowd. He was more than a head taller than anyone else. "Look closely at the man the LORD has chosen!" Samuel told the crowd. "There is no one like him!"

The crowd shouted, "Long live the king!"

Based on 1 Samuel 8.4, 5; 10.17-24

*"Look closely at the man the LORD has chosen!
There is no one like him!"*

"Samuel, we want a king to lead us."

"The LORD will choose your king."

Each tribe came to the altar.

Saul was chosen.

"Where is Saul?"

Samuel Has Surprising News for David

King Saul disobeyed the LORD over and over again and did things only for himself. Finally, the LORD decided that Saul was not able to be king of Israel.

So the LORD told Samuel the prophet, "Put some olive oil in a small container and go visit a man named Jesse, who lives in Bethlehem. I've chosen one of his sons to be my king. Take a calf with you and tell everyone that you've come to offer it as a sacrifice to me, then invite Jesse to the sacrifice." Samuel did what the LORD told him and went to Bethlehem.

When Jesse and his sons arrived, Samuel noticed Jesse's oldest son. "He has to be the one the LORD has chosen," Samuel said to himself.

But the LORD told him, "Samuel, don't think this man is the one just because he's tall and handsome. He isn't the one I've chosen. People judge others by what they look like, but I judge people by what is in their hearts."

One by one, Jesse had his seven sons go over to Samuel. Finally, Samuel said, "Jesse, the LORD hasn't chosen any of them. Do you have any more sons?"

"Yes," Jesse answered. "My youngest son David is out taking care of the sheep."

"Send for him!" Samuel said. "We won't start the ceremony until he gets here." Jesse sent for David. He was a healthy, good-looking boy with a sparkle in his eyes.

As soon as David came, the LORD told Samuel, "He's the one! Get up and pour the olive oil on his head." Samuel poured the oil on David's head while his brothers watched. At that moment, the Spirit of the LORD took control of David and stayed with him from then on. Samuel returned home.

Based on 1 Samuel 16.1-13

The LORD said, "People judge others by what they look like, but I judge people by what is in their hearts."

God told Samuel that Saul would no longer be king.

God sent Samuel to Jesse's house.

"Jesse, I want to meet all your sons."

Not one of Jesse's sons there was to be king.

"Do you have any other sons?"

"My youngest son David takes care of the sheep."

With Nothing but a Sling

The Philistines got ready for war and brought their troops together to attack the Israelites. The Philistine army had a hero named Goliath. He wore a bronze helmet and had bronze armor to protect his chest and legs. The chest armor alone weighed about one hundred twenty-five pounds.

Goliath went out and shouted to the army of Israel, "Choose your best soldier to come out and fight me!"

Goliath came out and gave his challenge every morning and every evening for forty days. When the Israelite soldiers saw Goliath, they were scared and ran off. They said to each other, "Look how he keeps coming out to insult us. The king is offering a big reward to the man who kills Goliath."

David asked some soldiers standing nearby, "Who does that worthless Philistine think he is? He's making fun of the army of the living God!"

Some soldiers overheard David talking, so they told Saul what David had said. Saul sent for David, and David came. "Your Majesty," he said, "this Philistine shouldn't turn us into cowards. I'll go out and fight him myself!"

Saul had his own military clothes and armor put on David, and he gave David a bronze helmet to wear. David strapped on a sword and tried to walk around, but he was not used to wearing those things.

So David took off the armor and picked up his shepherd's stick. He went out to a stream and picked up five smooth rocks and put them in his leather bag. Then with his sling in his hand, he went straight toward Goliath.

When Goliath saw that David was just a healthy, good-looking boy, he made fun of him. "Do you think I'm a dog?" Goliath asked. "Is that why you've come after me with a stick?"

David answered, "You've come out to fight me with a sword and a spear and a dagger. But I've come out to fight you in the name of the LORD All-Powerful. He is the God of Israel's army, and you have insulted him too! Today the LORD will help me defeat you."

When Goliath started forward, David ran toward him. He put a rock in his sling and swung the sling around by its straps. When he let go of one strap, the rock flew out and hit Goliath on the forehead. He fell facedown on the ground. David defeated Goliath with a sling and a rock.

Based on 1 Samuel 17.1-50

David told Goliath, "Today the LORD will help me defeat you."

Goliath and his army came to attack Israel.

Day after day Goliath made fun of Israel's God.

The Israelites were afraid of the giant Goliath.

David was not afraid.

David could not move.

David used his sling to kill Goliath.

God helped David defeat Goliath.

Solomon Chooses Wisdom

One night, the LORD God appeared to King Solomon in a dream and said, "Ask for anything you want, and I will give it to you."

Solomon answered, "My father David, your servant, was honest and did what you commanded. You were always loyal to him, and you gave him a son who is now king. LORD God, I'm your servant, and you've made me king in my father's place. But I'm very young and know so little about being a leader. Please make me wise and teach me the difference between right and wrong."

God said, "Solomon, I'm pleased that you asked for this. So I'll make you wiser than anyone who has ever lived or ever will live. I'll also give you what you didn't ask for. You'll be rich and respected as long as you live, and you'll be greater than any other king. If you obey me and follow my commands, as your father David did, I'll let you live a long time."

Solomon woke up and realized that God had spoken to him in the dream. God made Solomon brilliant and blessed him with insight and understanding. He was wiser than anyone else in the world, including the wisest people of the east and of Egypt. Solomon became famous in every country around Judah and Israel.

Solomon wrote three thousand wise sayings and composed more than one thousand songs. He could talk about all kinds of plants, from large trees to small bushes, and he taught about animals, birds, reptiles, and fish. Kings all over the world heard about Solomon's wisdom and sent people to listen to him teach.

Based on 1 Kings 3, 4

God said, "Solomon, I'll make you wiser than anyone who has ever lived or ever will live."

God spoke to Solomon, "Ask me for anything."

Solomon said, "Please make me wise."

"Teach me the difference between right and wrong."

Solomon realized God came to him in a dream.

People came from everywhere to learn from Solomon.

Solomon wrote wise sayings and composed songs.

Building God's House

King Solomon said to the king of Tyre, "The LORD God promised my father David that when his son became king, he would build a temple for worshiping the LORD. So I've decided to do that. I'd like you to have your workers cut down cedar trees for me. We both know your workers are more experienced than anyone else at cutting lumber."

Solomon also had workers cut stone in the hill country of Israel. He ordered other workers to cut and shape the blocks of stone for the foundation of the temple.

Solomon's workers started building the temple four years after Solomon became king of Israel. Seven years later they finished it, exactly as it had been planned.

Solomon then decided to have the sacred chest moved to the temple from Mount Zion. He called together the leaders of Israel. The priests and the Levites carried the sacred chest to the temple. Solomon and a crowd of people walked in front of the chest. The priests carried the chest into the most holy place and put it under the winged creatures.

Suddenly a cloud filled the temple as the priests were leaving the most holy place. The LORD's glory was in the cloud, and the light from it was so bright that the priests could not stay inside to do their work. Then Solomon prayed:

"Our LORD, you said that you
would live in a dark cloud.
Now I have built a glorious temple
where you can live forever."

Based on 1 Kings 5.5—8.13

Solomon prayed, "I have built a glorious temple where you can live forever."

"I am planning to build God's temple."

Solomon asked the king of Tyre for help.

So the king had his workers cut down trees…

and shape stones.

They worked seven years to complete the temple.

Solomon moved the sacred chest to the temple.

God was now in the temple.

Solomon gave thanks.

Plenty of Oil and Flour

Once there was no rain in Israel and the farmers could not grow enough to feed the people. So the LORD told his prophet Elijah, "Go to a town in northern Israel and live there. I've told a widow in that town to give you food."

When Elijah came near the town gate, he saw a widow gathering sticks for a fire. "Would you please bring me a cup of water?" he asked. As she left to get it, he asked, "Would you also please bring me a piece of bread?"

The widow answered, "In the name of the living LORD your God, I swear that I don't have any bread. All I have is a handful of flour and a little olive oil. I'm on my way home now with these few sticks to cook what I have for my son and me. After that, we will starve to death."

Elijah said, "Everything will be fine. Do what you said. Go home and fix something for you and your son. But first, please make a small piece of bread and bring it to me. The LORD God of Israel has promised that your jar of flour won't run out and your bottle of oil won't dry up before he sends rain for the crops."

The widow went home and did exactly what Elijah had told her. She and Elijah and her family had enough food for a long time. The LORD kept the promise that his prophet Elijah had made, and she did not run out of flour or oil.

Based on 1 Kings 17.8-16

When the widow obeyed, the LORD kept the promise
that his prophet Elijah had made to her.

God sent Elijah to a town in northern Israel.

God told a widow there to give him food.

Elijah asked her for a cup of water.

Elijah told the widow to bake bread.

"God promises to give you all the oil and flour you need."

The widow and her son always had food.

More Power for Elisha

One day Elijah said to Elisha, "The LORD wants me to go to the Jordan River, but you must stay here."

Elisha replied, "I swear by the living LORD and by your own life that I will never leave you!" So the two of them walked on together.

Fifty prophets followed Elijah and Elisha, then stood at a distance and watched as the two men walked toward the river. When they got there, Elijah took off his coat, then he rolled it up and struck the water with it. At once a path opened up through the river, and the two of them walked across on dry ground. After they had reached the other side, Elijah said, "Elisha, the LORD will soon take me away. What can I do for you before that happens?"

Elisha answered, "Please give me twice as much of your power as you give the other prophets, so I can be the one who takes your place as their leader."

"It won't be easy," Elijah answered. "It can happen only if you see me as I am being taken away."

Elijah and Elisha were walking along and talking, when suddenly there appeared between them a flaming chariot pulled by fiery horses. Right away, a strong wind took Elijah up into heaven. After Elijah had gone, Elisha tore his clothes in sorrow.

Elijah's coat had fallen off, so Elisha picked it up and walked back to the Jordan River. He struck the water with the coat. As soon as Elisha did this, a dry path opened up through the water, and he walked across.

When the prophets from Jericho saw what happened, they said to each other, "Elisha now has Elijah's power."

Based on 2 Kings 2.6-15

Suddenly there appeared between Elijah and Elisha a flaming chariot pulled by fiery horses. A strong wind took Elijah up into heaven.

God told Elijah and Elisha to go to the Jordan River.

Fifty prophets followed them.

The river parted!

"Give me twice as much of your power."

"It will happen when God takes me away."

A strong wind took Elijah to heaven.

Elijah's coat was left behind.

Elisha struck the river and it parted.

The prophets knew Elisha had Elijah's power.

Wash Seven Times and Be Healed

Naaman was the commander of the Syrian army. The Lord had helped him and his troops defeat their enemies, so the king of Syria respected Naaman very much. Naaman was a brave soldier, but he had leprosy.

One day while the Syrian troops were raiding Israel, they captured a girl, and she became a servant of Naaman's wife. Some time later the girl said, "If your husband Naaman would go to the prophet in Samaria, he would be cured of his leprosy."

So Naaman took his horses and chariots and went to Samaria. He went to the prophet Elisha's house. Elisha sent someone outside to say to him, "Go wash seven times in the Jordan River. Then you'll be completely cured."

But Naaman stormed off, grumbling, "Why couldn't he come out and talk to me? I thought for sure he would stand in front of me and pray to the Lord his God, then wave his hand over my skin and cure me. What about the two rivers close to my home in Damascus? They are just as good as any river in Israel. I could have washed in them and been cured."

His servants went over to him and said, "Sir, if the prophet had told you to do something difficult, you would have done it. So why don't you do what he said? Go wash and be cured."

Naaman walked down to the Jordan; he waded out into the water and stooped down in it seven times, just as Elisha had told him. Right away, he was cured, and his skin became as smooth as a child's.

Naaman and his officials went back to Elisha. Naaman stood in front of him and announced, "Now I know that the God of Israel is the only God in the whole world."

Based on 2 Kings 5.1-15

Naaman waded out into the Jordan River and stooped down in it seven times, just as Elisha had told him.

Naaman had a skin disease.

"Elisha the prophet can heal your husband."

Naaman's wife told him the good news.

Naaman went to Elisha . . .

but Elisha refused to see him.

"Elisha says to wash seven times in the Jordan River."

"Why can't I wash in a river close to my home?"

Naaman finally did what Elisha had said.

He washed seven times in the river.

Namaan was healed!

Cleaning God's Temple

Hezekiah was twenty-five years old when he became king of Judah. He obeyed the Lord by doing right, just as his ancestor David had done.

In the first month that King Hezekiah ruled Judah, he unlocked the doors to the Lord's temple and had them repaired. Then he called all the priests to the east courtyard of the temple and said, "It's time to purify the temple of the Lord God of our ancestors. You must first go through the ceremony to make yourselves clean, then go into the temple and bring out everything that is unclean and unacceptable to the Lord. Some of our ancestors were unfaithful and disobeyed the Lord our God. They also completely ignored his temple. So I have decided to renew our agreement with the Lord God of Israel."

The priests all went through the ceremony to make themselves clean. Then they began to purify the temple according to the Law of the Lord, just as Hezekiah had commanded.

After offering sacrifices to the Lord, Hezekiah and the crowd of worshipers knelt down and worshiped the Lord. Then Hezekiah and his officials ordered the priests to sing songs of praise to the Lord.

So the temple was once again used for worshiping the Lord. Hezekiah and the people of Judah celebrated, because God had helped them make this happen so quickly.

Based on 2 Chronicles 29.1-36

So the temple was once again used for worshiping the LORD.

King Hezekiah was only 25 years old when he became king.

He obeyed God and wanted to do what was right.

The temple was not being used to worship God.

King Hezekiah unlocked the doors to the temple.

Then he commanded the priests to clean out the temple.

Jerusalem Is Destroyed

Year after year, the kings and the people of Judah had disobeyed the LORD God of Israel and worshiped foreign gods. The prophets warned them that the LORD would soon punish them. Finally, it happened just as the prophets had said.

So the LORD sent King Nebuchadnezzar of Babylonia to attack Jerusalem. Nebuchadnezzar killed the young men who were in the temple, and he showed no mercy to anyone, whether man or woman, young or old. God let him kill everyone in the city.

Nebuchadnezzar carried off everything that was left in the temple; he robbed the treasury and the personal storerooms of the king and his officials. He took everything back to his capital in Babylon. Nebuchadnezzar's troops burned down the temple and destroyed every important building in the city. Then they broke down the city wall. The survivors were taken to Babylonia as prisoners, where they were slaves of the king and his sons.

Judah was an empty desert, and it stayed that way for seventy years.

Based on 2 Chronicles 36.17-21

Judah was an empty desert, and it stayed that way for seventy years.

The people of Judah disobeyed God, so God decided to punish them.

God let a foreign king attack Jerusalem.

Many people of Jerusalem were captured.

The king carried off everything in God's temple.

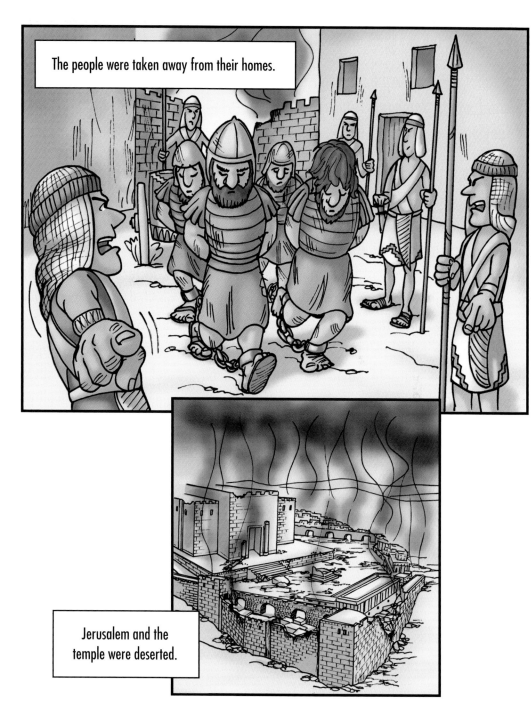

The people were taken away from their homes.

Jerusalem and the temple were deserted.

A Foreign King Helps God's People

Years ago the LORD had promised the prophet Jeremiah that the people of Israel would someday return home to Jerusalem from their captivity in Babylonia.

The LORD kept this promise and had the king of Persia send this official message to all parts of his kingdom, "I am King Cyrus of Persia. The LORD God of heaven, who is also the God of Israel, has made me the ruler of all nations on earth. And he has chosen me to build a temple for him in Jerusalem. The LORD God will watch over and encourage any of his people who want to go back to Jerusalem and help build the temple. Everyone else must provide what is needed. They must give money, supplies, and animals, as well as gifts for rebuilding God's temple."

Many people felt that the LORD God wanted them to help rebuild his temple, and they made plans to go to Jerusalem. The others helped by giving silver articles, gold, personal possessions, cattle, and other valuable gifts, as well as offerings for the temple.

King Cyrus gave back the things that Nebuchadnezzar had taken from the LORD's temple in Jerusalem. Everyone returned to the towns from which their families had come, including the priests, their helpers, the musicians, the temple guards, and the workers.

Based on Ezra 1.1-7; 2.70

Everyone returned to the towns from which their families had come.

"I, King Cyrus, will let the people of Israel return home."

"And I will help you rebuild God's temple in Jerusalem."

The king gave back everything taken from the temple.

He also gave money to help rebuild the temple.

The Israelites made plans to return to Jerusalem.

They took gifts for the temple.

They were happy to be home.

Jerusalem's Walls Stand Again!

I am Nehemiah, and I live in the country of Persia where I serve the king. One day, I heard that the walls of Jerusalem needed rebuilding. When I heard this, I sat down and cried.

The king said to me, "Why do you look so sad?"

I answered, "Your Majesty, I feel sad because the city where my ancestors are buried is in ruins, and its gates have been burned down. Sir, if it's all right with you, please send me back to Judah, so that I can rebuild the city of Jerusalem."

The king agreed to let me go, and I told him when I would return.

Three days after arriving in Jerusalem, I got up during the night and left my house on a donkey. As I rode along, I took a good look at the crumbled walls of the city and the gates that had been torn down and burned.

None of the city officials knew what I had in mind. But when I got back, I said to them, "Jerusalem is truly in a mess! The gates have been torn down and burned, and everything is in ruins. We must rebuild the city wall so that we can again take pride in our city."

Then I told them how kind God had been and what the king had said. Immediately, they replied, "Let's start building now!" So they got everything ready.

Three leaders heard about our plans and started insulting us and saying, "Just look at you! Do you plan to rebuild the walls of the city and rebel against the king?"

I answered, "We are servants of the God who rules from heaven, and he will make our work succeed. So we will start rebuilding Jerusalem."

It took us fifty-two days to rebuild the walls. When our enemies in the surrounding nations learned that the work was finished, they felt helpless, because they knew that our God had helped us rebuild the wall.

Based on Nehemiah 1; 2; 6.15,16

Nehemiah went to inspect the walls.

"It's time to rebuild the walls."

The people rejoiced.

Esther's Courage Saves Her People

The king of Persia had chosen a Jewish woman named Esther to be his queen. Her uncle Mordecai refused to bow down to Haman, one of the king's officials. When Haman found out that Mordecai was Jewish, he made plans to punish every Jew in the kingdom. Mordecai heard about this plan and convinced Esther to talk with the king, even though anyone who approached him without permission would be punished.

Esther dressed in her royal robes and went to the king's throne. She was relieved the king was happy to see her. He asked, "Esther, what brings you here?"

Esther said, "Please come with Haman to a dinner I will prepare."

Later that day, while the king and Haman were dining with Esther, the king said, "Esther, what can I do for you? Just ask, and I will give you as much as half of my kingdom!"

Esther answered, "Your Majesty, if you really care for me and are willing to help, you can save me and my people. That's what I really want, because a reward has been promised to anyone who kills my people."

"Who would dare to do such a thing?" the king asked.

Esther replied, "That evil Haman is the one out to get us!" Haman was terrified, as he looked at the king and the queen.

The king was so angry that he got up, left his wine, and went out into the palace garden. Haman realized that the king had already decided what to do with him, and he stayed and begged Esther to save his life. The king came back into the room and ordered Haman to be sent away. Then he wrote a law allowing the Jews to defend themselves and to protect their families and homes.

Based on Esther 5.1-4; 7–8

Esther answered, "Your Majesty, if you really care for me and are willing to help, you can save me and my people."

A Jewish woman named Esther was chosen to be the queen of Persia.

Her uncle Mordecai refused to bow down, so Haman decided to punish every Jew in the kingdom.

Mordecai heard about Haman's plan.

198

Esther asked to have dinner with the king and Haman.

"Haman has made plans to destroy the Jews—my own people!"

The king made a law to let the Jews defend themselves.

The Jews were saved because of Esther's courage.

A Happy Ending to a Sad Story

Job was a truly good person who respected God and refused to do evil. He had a large family and owned a lot of cattle and sheep. He was the richest person in the East.

One day, Job's sons and daughters were having a feast in the home of his oldest son, when someone rushed up to Job and said, "While your servants were plowing with your oxen, and your donkeys were nearby eating grass, a gang attacked and stole the oxen and donkeys! Your other servants were killed, and I was the only one who escaped to tell you."

That servant was still speaking, when a second one came running up and saying, "God sent down a fire that killed your sheep and your servants. I am the only one who escaped to tell you."

Before that servant finished speaking, a third one raced up and said, "Three gangs attacked and stole your camels! All of your other servants were killed, and I am the only one who escaped to tell you."

That servant was still speaking, when a fourth one dashed up and said, "Your children were having a feast and drinking wine at the home of your oldest son, when suddenly a windstorm from the desert blew the house down, crushing all of your children. I am the only one who escaped to tell you."

When Job heard this, he tore his clothes and shaved his head because of his great sorrow. He knelt on the ground, then worshiped God and said, "We bring nothing at birth; we take nothing with us at death. The LORD alone gives and takes. Praise the name of the LORD!"

In spite of everything, Job did not sin or accuse God of doing wrong. So the LORD made Job twice as rich as he was before.

Based on Job 1.1-22; 42.10

In spite of everything, Job did not sin or accuse God of doing wrong.

Job had a lot of children and cattle. But one day he got terrible news.

"Your donkeys were stolen and your sheep are dead."

202

Job refused to blame God...

but continued to worship God.

God blessed Job!

The Good Shepherd

You, LORD, are my shepherd. I will never be in need.
   You let me rest in fields of green grass.
You lead me to streams of peaceful water,
   and you refresh my life.

You are true to your name,
   and you lead me along the right paths.
I may walk through valleys as dark as death,
   but I won't be afraid.
You are with me,
   and your shepherd's rod makes me feel safe.

You treat me to a feast, while my enemies watch.
You honor me as your guest,
   and you fill my cup until it overflows.
Your kindness and love will always be with me
each day of my life,
   and I will live forever in your house, LORD.

Based on Psalm 23

You, LORD, are my shepherd. I will never be in need.

God is like a shepherd caring for his sheep.

We rest in fields of green grass.

God leads us to peaceful water.

God protects us.

God treats us like a special guest.

God's love will always be with us.

Praise God!

Shout praises to the LORD! Praise God in his temple.
　　Praise God in heaven, his mighty fortress.
Praise our God!
　　God's deeds are wonderful, too marvelous to describe.

Praise God with trumpets and all kinds of harps.
Praise God with tambourines and dancing,
　　with stringed instruments and woodwinds.
Praise God with cymbals, with clashing cymbals.
Let every living creature praise the LORD.
　　Shout praises to the LORD!

Based on Psalm 150

Shout praises to the LORD!

Shout praises to God.

Praise God with trumpets and harps.

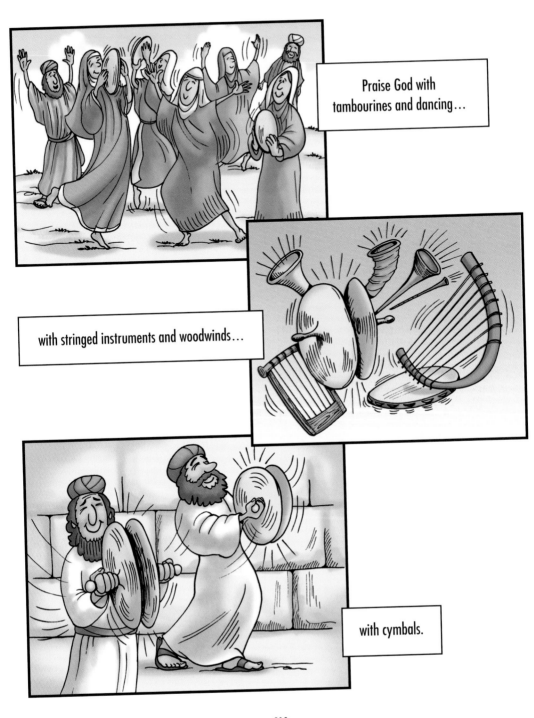

Let every living creature praise God.

Stay Away from Bad Friends

My child, obey the teachings of your parents,
and wear their teachings as you would a lovely hat
    or a pretty necklace.
Don't be tempted by sinners or listen when they say,
"Come on! Let's gang up and kill somebody,
    just for the fun of it!
They're well and healthy now,
    but we'll finish them off once and for all.
We'll take their valuables
    and fill our homes with stolen goods.
If you join our gang, you'll get your share."

Don't follow anyone like that or do what they do.
They are in a big hurry to commit some crime,
    perhaps even murder.
They are like a bird that sees the bait,
    but ignores the trap.
They gang up to murder someone,
    but they are the victims.
The wealth you get from crime robs you of your life.

Based on Proverbs 1.8-19

Obey the teachings of your parents.

Listen to your parents.

213

Don't be tempted to hurt others.

Say no to doing wrong.

Watch What You Say and Do

The Lord hates cheating
    but likes when people do the honest thing.
Too much pride can put you to shame.
    It's wiser to be humble.
If you do the right thing, honesty will be your guide.
But if you are crooked,
    you will be trapped by your own dishonesty.

If you are truly good, you will do right;
    if you are wicked, you will be destroyed by your own sin.
Honesty can keep you safe,
    but if you can't be trusted, you trap yourself.

Dishonest people use gossip to destroy their neighbors;
    good people are protected by their own good sense.
It's stupid to say bad things about your neighbors.
    If you are sensible, you will keep quiet.
A gossip tells everything,
    but a true friend will keep a secret.

Kindness is rewarded—
    but if you are cruel, you hurt yourself.
Meanness gets you nowhere, but goodness is rewarded.
Always do the right thing, and you will live;
    keep on doing wrong, and you will die.

Good people want what is best,
    but troublemakers hope to stir up trouble.

Sometimes you can become rich by being generous
    or poor by being greedy.
Generosity will be rewarded: Give a cup of water,
    and you will receive a cup of water in return.
Try hard to do right, and you will win friends;
    go looking for trouble, and you will find it.
If good people are rewarded here on this earth,
    all who are cruel and mean will surely be punished.

Based on Proverbs 11

Try hard to do right, and you will win friends.

Be honest and don't lie.

Be good and do what's right.

Say kind things about others.

Just the Right Time

Everything on earth has its own time and its own season.
   There is a time for birth and death,
      planting and reaping,
      for killing and healing, destroying and building,
      for crying and laughing, weeping and dancing,
      for throwing stones and gathering stones,
      embracing and parting.
   There is a time for finding and losing,
      keeping and giving,
      for tearing and sewing, listening and speaking.
   There is also a time for love and hate,
      for war and peace.

Based on Ecclesiastes 3.1-8

Everything on earth has its own time and its own season.

Everything on earth has its season.

There is a time for birth and death.

There is a time for planting and reaping…

for destroying and building.

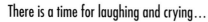

There is a time for laughing and crying…

for hellos and good-byes…

for listening and speaking.

Peace at Last

Like a branch that sprouts from a stump,
  someone from David's family will someday be king.
The Spirit of the Lord will be with him
  to give him understanding, wisdom, and insight.
He will be powerful, and he will know
  and honor the Lord.
His greatest joy will be to obey the Lord.

This king won't judge by appearances or listen to rumors.
The poor and the needy will be treated with fairness
  and with justice.
His word will be law everywhere in the land.
Honesty and fairness will be his royal robes.

Leopards will lie down with young goats,
  and wolves will rest with lambs.
Calves and lions will eat together
  and be cared for by little children.
Cows and bears will share the same pasture;
their young will rest side by side.
  Lions and oxen will both eat straw.

Little children will play near snake holes.
They will stick their hands into dens of poisonous snakes
    and never be hurt.

Nothing harmful will take place
    on the LORD's holy mountain.
Just as water fills the sea,
the land will be filled with people
    who know and honor the LORD.

Based on Isaiah 11.1-9

Someone from David's family will someday be king.

Our new king from David's family will come someday.

Our new king will obey God.

Our king will be fair to the poor.

Everything will be at peace.

Children will care for lions and calves.

Cows and bears will eat side by side.

Everyone will honor God.

The Lord Gives Strength

God asks, "Who compares with me?
    Is anyone my equal?"
Look at the evening sky! Who created the stars?
    Who gave them each a name?
    Who leads them like an army?
The Lord is so powerful that none of the stars
    are ever missing.

You people of Israel say, "God pays no attention to us!
    He doesn't care if we are treated unjustly."
But how can you say that?
    Don't you know? Haven't you heard?
The Lord is the eternal God, Creator of the earth.
He never gets weary or tired;
    his wisdom cannot be measured.
The Lord gives strength to those who are weary.
    Even young people get tired, then stumble and fall.
But those who trust the Lord will find new strength.
They will be strong like eagles soaring upward on wings;
    they will walk and run without getting tired.

Based on Isaiah 40.25-31

Those who trust the LORD will find new strength.

God created all the stars.

God takes care of the earth...

and helps those who are tired.

God makes them as strong as eagles.

They will walk and run without getting tired.

231

Bones Come Back to Life

I am Ezekiel the prophet. One day I felt the LORD's power take control of me, and his Spirit carried me to a valley full of bones. The LORD showed me all around, and everywhere I looked I saw bones that were dried out. He said, "Ezekiel, son of man, can these bones come back to life?"

I replied, "LORD God, only you can answer that."

He then told me to say:

Dry bones, listen to what the LORD is saying to you, "I, the LORD God, will put breath in you, and once again you will live. I will wrap you with muscles and skin and breathe life into you. Then you will know that I am the LORD."

I did what the LORD said, but before I finished speaking, I heard a rattling noise. The bones were coming together! I saw muscles and skin cover the bones, but they had no life in them.

The LORD said:

Ezekiel, now say to the wind, "The LORD God commands you to blow from every direction and to breathe life into these dead bodies, so they can live again."

As soon as I said this, the wind blew among the bodies, and they came back to life! They all stood up, and there were enough to make a large army.

The LORD said:

Ezekiel, the people of Israel are like dead bones. They complain that they are dried up and that they have no hope for the future. So tell them, "I, the LORD God, promise to open your graves and set you free. I will bring you back to Israel, and when that happens, you will realize that I am the LORD. My Spirit will give you breath, and you will live again. I will bring you home, and you will know that I have kept my promise. I, the LORD, have spoken."

Based on Ezekiel 37.1-14

"My Spirit will give you breath, and you will live again."

The people of Israel were led away.

These people are as helpless as dry bones.

God said, "These bones will come back to life!"

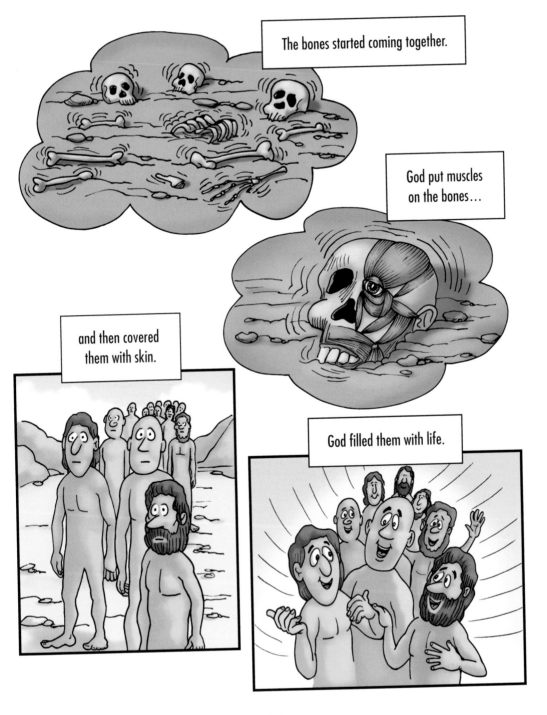

234

Daniel in a Pit with Lions

A foreign king put three men over his kingdom. One man was Daniel who did his work well and pleased the king. The other men tried to find something wrong with Daniel. But Daniel was honest and faithful and did everything he was supposed to do. Finally, they said to one another, "We will never be able to bring any charge against Daniel, unless it has to do with his religion."

They said to the king, "All of us agree that you should make a law forbidding anyone to pray to any god or human except you."

So the king made the law, but Daniel continued to pray to God just as he always had. The men who had spoken to the king saw Daniel praying and told the king, "Daniel refuses to obey you or the law that you ordered to be written. And he still prays to his god three times a day." The king was really upset to hear about this, and for the rest of the day he tried to think how he could save Daniel.

At sunset the men returned and said, "Your Majesty, remember that no written law can be changed, not even by the king." So the king ordered Daniel to be thrown into a pit of lions. But he said to Daniel, "You have been faithful to your God, and I pray that he will rescue you."

A stone was rolled over the pit. All night long the king could not sleep. At daybreak the king got up and ran to the pit. He shouted, "Daniel, you were faithful and served your God. Was he able to save you from the lions?"

Daniel answered, "My God knew that I was innocent and he kept the lions from eating me. Your Majesty, I have never done anything to hurt you." The king was relieved to hear Daniel's voice, and he gave orders for him to be taken out of the pit. Daniel's faith in his God had kept him from being harmed.

King Darius then sent this message to all people of every nation and race in the world, "Daniel's God has rescued him from the power of the lions."

Based on Daniel 6.1-27

Daniel's faith in his God had kept him from being harmed.

The king made Daniel an important leader.

The other leaders were jealous of Daniel.

"We need a law against praying to any god."

The king signed the law...

but Daniel kept praying.

Daniel was thrown into a pit with lions.

So God kept Daniel safe.

The king praised God for saving Daniel.

Jonah and a Big Fish

One day the LORD told Jonah to go to the great city of Nineveh and say to the people, "The LORD has seen your terrible sins!" Instead, Jonah ran from the LORD. He went to the seaport and bought a ticket on a ship. Then he got on the ship and sailed away to escape. But the LORD made a strong wind blow, and such a bad storm came up that the ship was about to be broken to pieces. The sailors were frightened, and they all started praying to their gods. They even threw the ship's cargo overboard to make the ship lighter.

All this time, Jonah was down below deck, sound asleep. The ship's captain went to him and said, "How can you sleep at a time like this? Get up and pray to your God! Maybe he will have pity on us and keep us from drowning."

Finally, the sailors got together and said, "Let's ask our gods to show us who caused all this trouble." It turned out to be Jonah.

The sailors were frightened because Jonah told them he was running from the LORD. Then they said, "Do you know what you have done?"

The storm kept getting worse, until finally the sailors asked him, "What should we do with you to make the sea calm down?"

Jonah told them, "Throw me into the sea, and it will calm down. I'm the cause of this terrible storm." So they threw Jonah overboard, and the sea calmed down.

The LORD sent a big fish to swallow Jonah, and Jonah was inside the fish for three days and three nights. From inside the fish, Jonah prayed to the LORD his God. Jonah asked God to save him.

The LORD commanded the fish to vomit up Jonah on the shore. And it did.

Once again the LORD told Jonah to go to that great city of Nineveh and preach his message of doom. Jonah obeyed the LORD and went to Nineveh.

Based on Jonah 1.1–3.3

The LORD sent a big fish to swallow Jonah.

God told Jonah to go to Nineveh.

Jonah sailed away instead.

So God sent a big storm.

"I am the cause of this storm."

So the sailors threw him into the sea.

Then the sea calmed.

A big fish swallowed Jonah.

He prayed for
God to save him.

The fish vomited Jonah onto the beach.

This time Jonah listened to God.

Good News for Israel

During the years that the people of Israel were held as captives in a foreign land, the prophet Zephaniah spoke these words:

Everyone in Jerusalem and Judah,
    celebrate and shout with all your heart!
Jerusalem, your punishment is over.
    The LORD has forced your enemies to turn and retreat.
Your LORD is King of Israel and stands at your side;
    you don't have to worry about any more troubles.

Jerusalem, the time is coming,
    when it will be said to you:
"Don't be discouraged or grow weak from fear!
The LORD your God wins victory after victory
    and is always with you.
God celebrates and sings because of you,
    and God will refresh your life with his love."

The LORD has promised:
Your sorrow has ended, and you can celebrate.
    I will punish those who mistreat you.
I will bring together the lame and the outcasts,
then they will be praised, instead of despised,
    in every country on earth.
I will lead you home, and with your own eyes
    you will see me bless you with all you once owned.
Then you will be famous everywhere on this earth.

Based on Zephaniah 3.14-20

The LORD has promised, "Your sorrow has ended, and you can celebrate."

"Let everyone be happy."

"God will take you home."

"God will bless Jerusalem."

New Testament

Mary Receives Good News

God sent the angel Gabriel to the town of Nazareth in Galilee with a message for a virgin named Mary. She was engaged to Joseph from the family of King David. The angel greeted Mary and said, "You are truly blessed! The Lord is with you."

Mary was confused by the angel's words and wondered what they meant. Then the angel told Mary, "Don't be afraid! God is pleased with you, and you will have a son. His name will be Jesus. He will be great and will be called the Son of God Most High. The LORD God will make him king, as his ancestor David was. He will rule the people of Israel forever, and his kingdom will never end."

Mary asked the angel, "How can this happen? I am not married!"

The angel answered, "The Holy Spirit will come down to you, and God's power will come over you. So your child will be called the holy Son of God. Your relative Elizabeth is also going to have a son, even though she is old. No one thought she could ever have a baby, but in three months she will have a son. Nothing is impossible for God!"

Mary said, "I am the Lord's servant! Let it happen as you have said." And the angel left her.

Based on Luke 1.26-38

The angel told Mary, "Don't be afraid! God is pleased with you, and you will have a son. His name will be Jesus."

God sent the angel Gabriel to Mary.

"God will bless you with a son."

"His name will be Jesus."

"How can this be? I'm not married."

"God will make it happen. Your child will be called God's son."

Jesus Is Born

Emperor Augustus gave orders for the names of all the people to be listed in record books. Everyone had to go to their own hometown to be listed. So Joseph had to leave Nazareth in Galilee and go to Bethlehem in Judea. Long ago Bethlehem had been King David's hometown, and Joseph went there because he was from David's family.

Mary was engaged to Joseph and traveled with him to Bethlehem. She was soon going to have a baby, and while they were there, she gave birth to a son. She dressed him in baby clothes and laid him on a bed of hay, because there was no room for them in the inn.

That night in the fields near Bethlehem some shepherds were guarding their sheep. All at once an angel came down to them from the Lord, and the brightness of the Lord's glory flashed around them. The shepherds were frightened. But the angel said, "Don't be afraid! I have good news for you. This very day in King David's hometown a Savior was born for you. He is Christ the Lord. You will know who he is, because you will find him dressed in baby clothes and lying on a bed of hay."

Suddenly many other angels came down from heaven and joined in praising God. They said: "Praise God in heaven! Peace on earth to everyone who pleases God."

After the angels had left and gone back to heaven, the shepherds said to each other, "Let's go to Bethlehem and see what the Lord has told us about." They hurried off and found Mary and Joseph, and they saw the baby lying on a bed of hay. As the shepherds returned to their sheep, they were praising God.

Eight days later Jesus' parents did for him what the Law of Moses commands. And they named him Jesus, just as the angel had told Mary when he promised she would have a baby.

Based on Luke 2.1-21

"This very day in King David's hometown a Savior was born for you. He is Christ the Lord."

Joseph and Mary went to Bethlehem to be counted.

But there was no room to stay in the inn.

So they stayed in the stable.

Mary gave birth to a baby boy.

Shepherds were nearby taking care of sheep.

An angel told them, "Don't be afraid. A Savior was born tonight in Bethlehem."

Suddenly a choir of angels began praising God.

"We must go see this baby."

The shepherds found the baby.

They returned to their sheep, praising God.

Wise Men Visit Jesus

When Jesus was born in the village of Bethlehem, Herod was king. During this time some wise men from the east came to Jerusalem and said, "Where is the child born to be king of the Jews? We saw his star in the east and have come to worship him."

When King Herod heard about this, he was worried, and so was everyone else in Jerusalem. Herod brought together the chief priests and the teachers of the Law of Moses and asked them, "Where will the Messiah be born?"

They told him, "He will be born in Bethlehem, just as the prophet wrote:

'Bethlehem in the land of Judea,
　　you are very important among the towns of Judea.
From your town will come a leader,
　　who will be like a shepherd for my people Israel.'"

Herod secretly called in the wise men and asked them when they had first seen the star. He told them, "Go to Bethlehem and search carefully for the child. As soon as you find him, let me know. I want to go and worship him too." The wise men listened to what the king said and then left. And the star they had seen in the east went on ahead of them until it stopped over the place where the child was. They were thrilled and excited to see the star.

When the men went into the house and saw the child with Mary, his mother, they knelt down and worshiped him. They took out their gifts of gold, frankincense, and myrrh and gave them to him. Later they were warned in a dream not to return to Herod, and they went back home by another road.

Based on Matthew 2.1-12

The wise men took out their gifts of gold, frankincense, and myrrh and gave them to the child.

Mary, Joseph, and Jesus lived in Bethlehem.

Wise men from the east followed a bright star to Jerusalem.

"King Herod, where is the baby who will be our king?"

The wise men followed the star to find Jesus.

The wise men gave gifts to Jesus.

They went home a different way to avoid seeing the king.

Jesus Amazes the Teachers in the Temple

Every year Jesus' parents went to Jerusalem for Passover. And when Jesus was twelve years old, they all went there as usual for the celebration. After Passover his parents left, but they did not know that Jesus had stayed on in the city.

They thought he was traveling with some other people, and they went a whole day before they started looking for him. When they could not find him with their relatives and friends, they went back to Jerusalem and started looking for him there. Three days later they found Jesus sitting in the temple, listening to the teachers and asking them questions. Everyone who heard him was surprised at how much he knew and at the answers he gave.

When his parents found him, they were amazed. His mother said, "Son, why have you done this to us? Your father and I have been very worried, and we have been searching for you!"

Jesus answered, "Why did you have to look for me? Didn't you know that I would be in my Father's house?" But they did not understand what he meant.

Jesus went back to Nazareth with his parents and obeyed them. His mother kept on thinking about all that had happened.

Jesus became wise, and he grew strong. God was pleased with him and so were the people.

Based Luke 2.41-52

Jesus answered, "Why did you have to look for me?
Didn't you know that I would be in my Father's house?"

Jesus and his parents went to Jerusalem.

They celebrated Passover together.

After the celebration, everyone returned home.

"Have you seen our son Jesus?"

Jesus had stayed to talk with the teachers in the temple.

They asked Jesus many questions.

He amazed them with his answers.

"We finally found you!"

"You should have known I would be teaching in the temple."

Mary never forgot what happened that day in the temple.

Jesus Is Baptized

John the Baptist started preaching in the desert of Judea. He said, "Turn back to God! The kingdom of heaven will soon be here."

John was the one the prophet Isaiah was talking about, when he said, "In the desert someone is shouting, 'Get the road ready for the Lord! Make a straight path for him.' "

John wore clothes made of camel's hair. He had a leather strap around his waist and ate grasshoppers and wild honey.

From Jerusalem and all Judea and from the Jordan River Valley crowds of people went to John. They told how sorry they were for their sins, and he baptized them in the river.

Jesus left Galilee and went to the Jordan River to be baptized by John. But John kept objecting and said, "I ought to be baptized by you. Why have you come to me?"

Jesus answered, "For now this is how it should be, because we must do all that God wants us to do." Then John agreed.

So Jesus was baptized. And as soon as he came out of the water, the sky opened, and he saw the Spirit of God coming down on him like a dove. Then a voice from heaven said, "This is my own dear Son, and I am pleased with him."

Based on Matthew 3.1-6, 13-17

A voice from heaven said, "This is my own dear Son, and I am pleased with him."

John preached about God's love.

"Live the way God wants you to live."

267

John baptized those who were sorry for their sins.

"Jesus, I cannot baptize you."

268

The Devil Tempts Jesus

After Jesus had been baptized, the power of the Holy Spirit was with him, and the Spirit led him into the desert. For forty days Jesus was tested by the devil, and during that time he went without eating. When it was all over, he was hungry.

The devil said to Jesus, "If you are God's Son, tell this stone to turn into bread."

Jesus answered, "The Scriptures say, 'No one can live only on food.' "

Then the devil led Jesus up to a high place and quickly showed him all the nations on earth. The devil said, "I will give all this power and glory to you. It has been given to me, and I can give it to anyone I want to. Just worship me, and you can have it all."

Jesus answered, "The Scriptures say, 'Worship the Lord your God and serve only him!' "

Finally, the devil took Jesus to Jerusalem and had him stand on top of the temple. The devil said, "If you are God's Son, jump off. The Scriptures say, 'God will tell his angels to take care of you. They will catch you in their arms, and you will not hurt your feet on the stones.' "

Jesus answered, "The Scriptures also say, 'Don't try to test the Lord your God!' "

After the devil had finished testing Jesus in every way possible, he left him for a while.

Based on Luke 4.1-13

*Jesus answered, "The Scriptures also say,
'Don't try to test the Lord your God!' "*

God led Jesus into the desert.

The devil came to test Jesus.

"If you are God's son, turn
the rock into bread."

271

"Jump down and have God's angels catch you."

"The Scriptures say not to test God!"

So the devil left Jesus alone.

A Surprising Catch!

Jesus was standing on the shore, teaching the people as they crowded around him to hear God's message. Near the shore he saw two boats left there by some fishermen who had gone to wash their nets. Jesus got into the boat that belonged to Peter and asked him to row it out a little way from the shore. Then Jesus sat down in the boat to teach the crowd.

When Jesus had finished speaking, he told Peter, "Row the boat out into the deep water and let your nets down to catch some fish."

"Master," Peter answered, "we have worked hard all night long and have not caught a thing. But if you tell me to, I will let the nets down." They did it and caught so many fish that their nets began ripping apart. Then they signaled for their partners in the other boat to come and help them. The men came, and together they filled the two boats so full that they both began to sink.

When Peter saw this happen, he knelt down in front of Jesus and said, "Lord, don't come near me! I am a sinner." Peter and everyone with him were completely surprised at all the fish they had caught. His partners James and John were surprised too.

Jesus told Peter, "Don't be afraid! From now on you will bring in people instead of fish." The men pulled their boats up on the shore. Then they left everything and went with Jesus.

Based on Luke 5.1-11

The men pulled their boats up on the shore.
Then they left everything and went with Jesus.

Jesus taught God's message.

Jesus climbed into Peter's boat...

so he could teach
the large crowd.

Later, Jesus told Peter to fish in the deep water.

"We already fished there, but I'll do what you say."

He caught more fish than the net could hold.

"I should have believed you."

"From now on, you will help me bring in people."

The fishermen left everything to follow Jesus.

Jesus Changes Water into Wine

Mary, the mother of Jesus, was at a wedding feast in the village of Cana in Galilee. Jesus and his disciples had also been invited and were there.

When the wine was all gone, Mary said to Jesus, "They don't have any more wine."

Jesus replied, "Mother, my time hasn't yet come! You must not tell me what to do."

Mary then said to the servants, "Do whatever Jesus tells you to do."

At the feast there were six stone water jars that were used by the people for washing themselves in the way that their religion said they must. Each jar held about twenty or thirty gallons. Jesus told the servants to fill them to the top with water. Then after the jars had been filled, he said, "Now take some water and give it to the man in charge of the feast."

The servants did as Jesus told them, and the man in charge drank some of the water that had now turned into wine. He did not know where the wine had come from, but the servants did. He called the bridegroom over and said, "The best wine is always served first. Then after the guests have had plenty, the other wine is served. But you have kept the best until last!" This was Jesus' first miracle.

Based on John 2.1-11

The servants did as Jesus told them, and the man in charge drank some of the water that had now turned into wine.

Jesus and his mother went to a wedding.

Soon Mary told Jesus that all the wine was gone.

The servants knew Jesus had turned the water into wine.

This was Jesus' first miracle.

Jesus Heals a Man

Jesus went back to Capernaum, and a few days later people heard that he was at home. Then so many of them came to the house that there wasn't even standing room left in front of the door.

Jesus was still teaching when four people came up, carrying a crippled man on a mat. But because of the crowd, they could not get him to Jesus. So they made a hole in the roof above him and let the man down in front of everyone.

When Jesus saw how much faith they had, he said to the crippled man, "My friend, your sins are forgiven."

Some of the teachers of the Law of Moses were sitting there. They started wondering, "Why would he say such a thing? He must think he is God! Only God can forgive sins."

Right away, Jesus knew what they were thinking, and he said, "Why are you thinking such things? Is it easier for me to tell this crippled man that his sins are forgiven or to tell him to get up and pick up his mat and go on home? I will show you that the Son of Man has the right to forgive sins here on earth." So Jesus said to the man, "Get up! Pick up your mat and go on home."

The man got right up. He picked up his mat and went out while everyone watched in amazement. They praised God and said, "We have never seen anything like this!"

Based on Mark 2.1-12

Jesus said to the lame man, "Get up! Pick up your mat and go on home." The man got right up.

Jesus was teaching inside a friend's home.

Some men brought their friend to see Jesus.

"It's too crowded to get inside!"

They made a hole in the roof and lowered him into the crowd.

"Your sins are forgiven."

Some thought, "Only God can forgive sins."

Jesus Calms the Storm

One evening, Jesus said to his disciples, "Let's cross to the east side." So they left the crowd, and his disciples started across the lake with him in the boat. Some other boats followed along. Suddenly a windstorm struck the lake. Waves started splashing into the boat, and it was about to sink.

Jesus was in the back of the boat with his head on a pillow, and he was asleep. His disciples woke him and said, "Teacher, don't you care that we're about to drown?"

Jesus got up and ordered the wind and the waves to be quiet. The wind stopped, and everything was calm.

Jesus asked his disciples, "Why were you afraid? Don't you have any faith?"

Now they were more afraid than ever and said to each other, "Who is this? Even the wind and the waves obey him!"

Based on Mark 4.35-41

Jesus asked his disciples, "Why were you afraid? Don't you have any faith?"

Jesus and his disciples were crossing the lake.

Suddenly a storm came.

The boat was about to sink.

"Jesus is asleep."

"We're about to drown. Help us!"

"Why are you so afraid?"

Jesus calmed the storm.

Even the wind and waves listened to Jesus!

Jesus Teaches How To Pray

When you pray, don't talk on and on as people do who don't know God. They think God likes to hear long prayers. Don't be like them. Your Father knows what you need before you ask.

You should pray like this:

Our Father in heaven,
     help us to honor your name.
Come and set up your kingdom,
so that everyone on earth will obey you,
     as you are obeyed in heaven.
Give us our food for today.
Forgive us for doing wrong,
     as we forgive others.
Keep us from being tempted
     and protect us from evil.

Based on Matthew 6.7-13

Our Father in heaven, help us to honor your name.

Jesus taught the people how to pray.

292

Jesus Teaches about God's Kingdom

Jesus used stories when he spoke to the people. In fact, he did not tell them anything without using stories.

A Hidden Treasure

The kingdom of heaven is like what happens when someone finds a treasure hidden in a field and buries it again. A person like that is happy and goes and sells everything in order to buy that field.

A Valuable Pearl

The kingdom of heaven is like what happens when a shop owner is looking for fine pearls. After finding a very valuable one, the owner goes and sells everything in order to buy that pearl.

A Fish Net

The kingdom of heaven is like what happens when a net is thrown into a lake and catches all kinds of fish. When the net is full, it is dragged to the shore, and the fishermen sit down to separate the fish. They keep the good ones, but throw the bad ones away. That's how it will be at the end of time. Angels will come and separate the evil people from the ones who have done right.

Jesus asked his disciples if they understood these things. They said, "Yes, we do."

Based on Matthew 13.34, 44-49, 51

Jesus used stories when he spoke to the people.

Jesus told stories to teach about God's kingdom.

"God's kingdom is like finding a buried treasure…

then selling everything to buy the field."

"God's kingdom is like finding an expensive pearl…

and selling everything to buy it."

Jesus Walks on Water

One day after teaching the crowds, Jesus made his disciples get into the boat and start back across the lake. But he stayed until he had sent the crowds away. Then he told them good-by and went up on the side of a mountain to pray.

Later that evening he was still there by himself, and the boat was somewhere in the middle of the lake. He could see that the disciples were struggling hard, because they were rowing against the wind. Not long before morning, Jesus came toward them. He was walking on the water and was about to pass the boat.

When the disciples saw Jesus walking on the water, they thought he was a ghost, and they started screaming. All of them saw him and were terrified. But at that same time he said, "Don't worry! I am Jesus. Don't be afraid."

He then got into the boat with them, and the wind died down.

Based on Mark 6.45-51

"I am Jesus. Don't be afraid."

Jesus' disciples set sail.

But soon a wind came over the lake.

The disciples were rowing hard.

Jesus walked toward the boat.

The disciples thought he was a ghost.

"I am Jesus. Don't be afraid."

Jesus got into the boat.

The winds calmed.

Jesus Heals a Girl

Everyone had been waiting for Jesus, and when he came back, a crowd was there to welcome him. Just then the man in charge of the Jewish meeting place came and knelt down in front of Jesus. His name was Jairus, and he begged Jesus to come to his home because his twelve-year-old child was dying. She was his only daughter.

Before Jesus could go to Jairus' home, someone came from his home and said, "Your daughter has died! Why bother the teacher anymore?"

When Jesus heard this, he said, "Don't worry! Have faith, and your daughter will get well."

Jesus went into the house, but he did not let anyone else go with him, except Peter, John, James, and the girl's father and mother. Everyone was crying and weeping for the girl. But Jesus said, "The child isn't dead. She is just asleep." The people laughed at him because they knew she was dead.

Jesus took hold of the girl's hand and said, "Child, get up!" She came back to life and got right up.

Based on Luke 8.40-42, 49-55

Jesus took hold of the girl's hand and said,
"Child, get up!" She came back to life and got right up.

A religious leader was trying to see Jesus.

"Please heal my daughter."

"Come with me."

"But your daughter has already died."

Jesus said, "Don't worry. She will get well."

"She's only sleeping—not dead."

The people laughed at what Jesus said.

"Child, get up."

The girl was alive again!

Jesus Feeds a Big Crowd

Jesus crossed Lake Galilee. A large crowd had seen him work miracles to heal the sick, and those people went with him. It was almost time for the Jewish festival of Passover, and Jesus went up on a mountain with his disciples and sat down.

When Jesus saw the large crowd coming toward him, he asked Philip, "Where will we get enough food to feed all these people?" He said this to test Philip, since he already knew what he was going to do.

Philip answered, "Don't you know that it would take almost a year's wages just to buy only a little bread for each of these people?"

Andrew, the brother of Simon Peter, was one of the disciples. He spoke up and said, "There is a boy here who has five small loaves of barley bread and two fish. But what good is that with all these people?"

The ground was covered with grass, and Jesus told his disciples to have everyone sit down. About five thousand men were in the crowd. Jesus took the bread in his hands and gave thanks to God. Then he passed the bread to the people, and he did the same with the fish, until everyone had plenty to eat.

The people ate all they wanted, and Jesus told his disciples to gather up the leftovers, so that nothing would be wasted. The disciples gathered them up and filled twelve large baskets with what was left over from the five barley loaves.

Based on John 6.1-13

Jesus passed the bread to the people, and he did the same with the fish, until everyone had plenty to eat.

A large crowd came to hear Jesus teach.

Jesus asked Philip, "Do we have enough to feed these people?"

"We don't have enough money to buy them food."

"Here's a boy with five loaves of bread and two fish."

Jesus told the disciples to have everyone sit down.

Jesus thanked God for the bread and fish.

Then the disciples passed
out the food to the crowd.

Everyone had plenty to eat.

And there was enough left
over to fill twelve baskets!

Jesus Heals a Sick Man

Jesus and his disciples sailed across Lake Galilee and came to shore near a town. As Jesus was getting out of the boat, he was met by a very sick man from that town. The man had demons in him.

The man saw Jesus and screamed. He knelt down in front of him and shouted, "Jesus, Son of God in heaven, what do you want with me? I beg you not to torture me!" He said this because Jesus had already told the evil spirit to go out of him.

The man had often been attacked by the demon. And even though he had been bound with chains and leg irons and kept under guard, he smashed whatever bound him. Then the demon would force him out into lonely places.

Jesus asked the man, "What is your name?"

He answered, "My name is Lots." He said this because there were 'lots' of demons in him. They begged Jesus not to send them to the deep pit, where they would be punished.

A large herd of pigs was feeding there on the hillside. So the demons begged Jesus to let them go into the pigs, and Jesus let them go. Then the demons left the man and went into the pigs. The whole herd rushed down the steep bank into the lake and drowned.

Then all who had seen the man healed told about it. Everyone from around the town begged Jesus to leave, because they were so frightened.

When Jesus got into the boat to start back, the man who had been healed begged to go with him. But Jesus sent him off and said, "Go back home and tell everyone how much God has done for you." The man then went all over town, telling everything that Jesus had done for him.

Based on Luke 8.26-39

Jesus sent the man off and said,
"Go back home and tell everyone how much God has done for you."

When Jesus and his disciples came to shore, a very sick man met them.

"Jesus, get away from me."

Jesus asked, "What is your name?"

"Lots," he replied because he had many evil spirits.

Jesus ordered the evil spirits to leave the man.

Jesus sent the evil spirits into the pigs.

Jesus completely healed him.

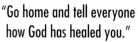

"Go home and tell everyone
how God has healed you."

Some people were still
afraid of the man.

But the man told
everyone his good news.

Being a Good Neighbor

Jesus told this story to a teacher about how we should treat others:

As a man was going down from Jerusalem to Jericho, robbers attacked him and grabbed everything he had. They beat him up and ran off, leaving him half dead.

A priest happened to be going down the same road. But when he saw the man, he walked by on the other side. Later a temple helper came to the same place. But when he saw the man who had been beaten up, he also went by on the other side.

A man from Samaria then came traveling along that road. When he saw the man, he felt sorry for him and went over to him. He treated his wounds with olive oil and wine and bandaged them. Then he put him on his own donkey and took him to an inn, where he took care of him. The next morning he gave the innkeeper two silver coins and said, "Please take care of the man. If you spend more than this on him, I will pay you when I return."

Then Jesus asked, "Which one of these three people was a real neighbor to the man who was beaten up by robbers?"
The teacher answered, "The one who showed pity."
Jesus said, "Go and do the same!"

Based on Luke 10.30-37

When he saw the man, he felt sorry for him and went over to him.

A man was traveling along a desert road.

He was attacked and beaten by robbers.

A priest passed him by.

A temple helper also passed by.

Then a man from another county stopped to help him.

This man bandaged his wounds.

He took him to an inn and paid the innkeeper to take care of him.

The Lost Sheep

Tax collectors and sinners were all crowding around to listen to Jesus. So the Pharisees and the teachers of the Law of Moses started grumbling, "This man is friendly with sinners. He even eats with them."

Then Jesus told them this story:

If any of you has a hundred sheep, and one of them gets lost, what will you do? Won't you leave the ninety-nine in the field and go look for the lost sheep until you find it? And when you find it, you will be so glad that you will put it on your shoulder and carry it home. Then you will call in your friends and neighbors and say, "Let's celebrate! I've found my lost sheep."

Jesus said, "In the same way there is more happiness in heaven because of one sinner who turns to God than over ninety-nine good people who don't need to."

Based on Luke 15.1-7

*Then you will call in your friends and neighbors and say,
"Let's celebrate! I've found my lost sheep."*

Jesus told a story about a lost sheep.

"A shepherd had 100 sheep."

"One day the shepherd discovered that one sheep was missing."

"The shepherd left his sheep to find the lost one."

"He searched everywhere."

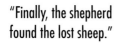
"Finally, the shepherd found the lost sheep."

"He carried the sheep home."

"And had a celebration!"

A Father's Love

Jesus told this story:

Once a man had two sons. The younger son said to his father, "Give me my share of the property." So the father divided his property between his two sons.

Not long after that, the younger son packed up everything he owned and left for a foreign country, where he wasted all his money in wild living. He had spent everything, when a bad famine spread through that whole land. Soon he had nothing to eat.

He went to work for a man in that country, and the man sent him out to take care of his pigs. He would have been glad to eat what the pigs were eating, but no one gave him a thing. Finally, he came to his senses and said, "My father's workers have plenty to eat, and here I am, starving to death! I will go to my father and say to him, 'Father, I have sinned against God in heaven and against you. I am no longer good enough to be called your son. Treat me like one of your workers.'"

The younger son got up and started back to his father. But when he was still a long way off, his father saw him and felt sorry for him. He ran to his son and hugged and kissed him. The son said, "Father, I have sinned against God in heaven and against you. I am no longer good enough to be called your son."

But his father said to the servants, "Hurry and bring the best clothes and put them on him. Give him a ring for his finger and sandals for his feet. Get the best calf and prepare it, so we can eat and celebrate. This son of mine was dead, but has now come back to life. He was lost and has now been found." And they began to celebrate.

Based on Luke 15.11-24

The loving father said, "This son of mine was dead, but has now come back to life. He was lost and has now been found."

Jesus told this story about a father and his son.

"The son asked for what belonged to him so he could run away."

"The son left for another country."

"He spent all his money on having fun."

"So now he was hungry."

"He thought about eating the pigs' food."

"Then the son remembered how well his father's servants were treated."

"So he decided to rush home."

"He was afraid his father would be upset...

but his father was happy to see him."

"He gave his son a robe and a ring, and everyone celebrated."

A Blind Man Meets Jesus

As Jesus and his disciples were going into a village, some people brought a blind man to him and begged him to touch the man. Jesus took him by the hand and led him out of the village, where he spit into the man's eyes. He placed his hands on the blind man and asked him if he could see anything. The man looked up and said, "I see people, but they look like trees walking around."

Once again Jesus placed his hands on the man's eyes, and this time the man stared. His eyes were healed, and he saw everything clearly. Jesus said to him, "You may return home now, but don't go into the village."

Based on Mark 8.22-26

The man's eyes were healed, and he saw everything clearly.

Jesus and his disciples walked toward a town.

A crowd of people met them.

Some people brought a blind man to Jesus.

Jesus spit on the man's eyes.

"What do you see?" Jesus asked.

Jesus Welcomes the Children

Some people brought their children to Jesus so that he could bless them by placing his hands on them. But his disciples told the people to stop bothering him.

When Jesus saw this, he became angry and said, "Let the children come to me! Don't try to stop them. People who are like these little children belong to the kingdom of God. I promise you that you cannot get into God's kingdom, unless you accept it the way a child does."

Then Jesus took the children in his arms and blessed them by placing his hands on them.

Based on Mark 10.13-16

"People who are like these little children belong to the kingdom of God."

Jesus was teaching his disciples.

Some people brought their children to Jesus.

The disciples tried to stop them.

"Let the children come to me."

Jesus talked to the children.

"I want people to be more like children."

Jesus blessed the children.

Jesus Rides a Donkey

Jesus was headed toward Jerusalem. As he was getting near the Mount of Olives, he sent two of his disciples on ahead. He told them, "Go into the next village, where you will find a young donkey that has never been ridden. Untie the donkey and bring it here. If anyone asks why you are doing that, just say, 'The Lord needs it.' "

They went off and found everything just as Jesus had said. While they were untying the donkey, its owners asked, "Why are you doing that?"

They answered, "The Lord needs it."

Then they led the donkey to Jesus. They put some of their clothes on its back and helped Jesus get on. And as he rode along, the people spread clothes on the road in front of him. When Jesus was starting down the Mount of Olives, his large crowd of disciples were happy and praised God because of all the miracles they had seen. They shouted,

> "Blessed is the king who comes in the name of the Lord!
>   Peace in heaven and glory to God."

Based on Luke 19.28-38

"Blessed is the king who comes in the name of the Lord!"

Jesus sent two disciples to get a donkey.

"The Lord needs to use your donkey."

They took the donkey back to Jesus.

Jesus rode the donkey toward Jerusalem.

A crowd began to shout praises.

"Blessed is Jesus our King!"

Mary Honors Jesus

Six days before the Jewish festival of Passover, Jesus went to visit his friends in Bethany. A meal had been prepared for Jesus. Martha was doing the serving, and Lazarus was there.

Mary took a very expensive bottle of perfume and poured it on Jesus' feet. She wiped them with her hair, and the sweet smell of the perfume filled the house.

A disciple named Judas was there, and he asked, "Why wasn't this perfume sold for three hundred silver coins and the money given to the poor?" Judas did not really care about the poor. He asked this because he carried the moneybag and sometimes would steal from it.

Jesus replied, "Leave her alone! She has kept this perfume for the day of my burial. You will always have the poor with you, but you won't always have me."

Based on John 12.1-8

Mary took a very expensive bottle of perfume and poured it on Jesus' feet.

Jesus was eating at Martha and Mary's house.

Martha prepared and served the food.

Mary brought in a bottle of perfume...

and poured it over Jesus' feet.

Judas asked, "Why waste expensive perfume?"

"Why not sell it and give
the money to the poor."

But Jesus knew Judas did
not care about the poor.

"Leave her alone.
She is honoring me."

341

Jesus Teaches about Serving

It was just before the Jewish festival of Passover, and Jesus knew that the time had come for him to leave this world and to return to the Father. He had always loved his followers in this world, and he loved them to the very end.

Jesus knew that he had come from God and would go back to God. He also knew that the Father had given him complete power. So during the meal Jesus got up, removed his outer garment, and wrapped a towel around his waist. He put some water into a large bowl. Then he began washing his disciples' feet and drying them with the towel he was wearing.

After Jesus had washed his disciples' feet and had put his outer garment back on, he sat down again. Then he said:

Do you understand what I have done? You call me your teacher and Lord, and you should, because that is who I am. And if your Lord and teacher has washed your feet, you should do the same for each other. I have set the example, and you should do for each other exactly what I have done for you. I tell you for certain that servants are not greater than their master, and messengers are not greater than the one who sent them. You know these things, and God will bless you, if you do them.

Based on John 13.1-5, 12-17

"I tell you for certain that servants are not greater than their master, and messengers are not greater than the one who sent them."

Jesus ate a meal with his disciples.

Jesus knew he would go back to God.

So he got up and removed his robe.

Jesus picked up a bowl.

Jesus Eats a Last Meal

When the time came for Jesus and the apostles to eat, he said to them, "I have very much wanted to eat this Passover meal with you before I suffer. I tell you that I will not eat another Passover meal until it is finally eaten in God's kingdom."

Jesus took a cup of wine in his hands and gave thanks to God. Then he told the apostles, "Take this wine and share it with each other. I tell you that I will not drink any more wine until God's kingdom comes."

Jesus took some bread in his hands and gave thanks for it. He broke the bread and handed it to his apostles. Then he said, "This is my body, which is given for you. Eat this as a way of remembering me!"

After the meal he took another cup of wine in his hands. Then he said, "This is my blood. It is poured out for you, and with it God makes his new agreement. The one who will betray me is here at the table with me! The Son of Man will die in the way that has been decided for him, but it will be terrible for the one who betrays him!"

Then the apostles started arguing about who would ever do such a thing.

Based on Luke 22.14-23

346

Jesus ate with his disciples.

"Drink this wine to remember God's promise."

"Soon one of you will turn against me."

The disciples wondered who would do that.

Jesus Prays in the Garden

One night Jesus went out to the Mount of Olives, as he often did, and his disciples went with him. When they got there, he told them, "Pray that you won't be tested."

Jesus walked on a little way before he knelt down and prayed, "Father, if you will, please don't make me suffer by having me drink from this cup. But do what you want, and not what I want."

Then an angel from heaven came to help him. Jesus was in great pain and prayed so sincerely that his sweat fell to the ground like drops of blood.

Jesus got up from praying and went over to his disciples. They were asleep and worn out from being so sad. He said to them, "Why are you asleep? Wake up and pray that you won't be tested."

Based on Luke 22.39-46

Jesus prayed, "Father, if you will, please don't make me suffer. But do what you want, and not what I want."

Jesus and his disciples went to the Mount of Olives.

"Ask God to give you strength."

"Stay awake and pray."

Jesus went to pray alone.

"I don't want to suffer."

"But I will do what you want."

Jesus said, "I know you're sad and tired, but you should be praying."

Jesus Is Arrested

While Jesus was speaking with his disciples, a crowd came up. It was led by Judas, one of the twelve apostles. He went over to Jesus and greeted him with a kiss.

Jesus asked Judas, "Are you betraying the Son of Man with a kiss?"

When Jesus' disciples saw what was about to happen, they asked, "Lord, should we attack them with a sword?" One of the disciples even struck at the high priest's servant with his sword and cut off the servant's right ear.

"Enough of that!" Jesus said. Then he touched the servant's ear and healed it.

Jesus spoke to the chief priests, the temple police, and the leaders who had come to arrest him. He said, "Why do you come out with swords and clubs and treat me like a criminal? I was with you every day in the temple, and you didn't arrest me. But this is your time, and darkness is in control."

Based on Luke 22.47-53

Jesus asked Judas, "Are you betraying the Son of Man with a kiss?"

Judas led the group that came to arrest Jesus.

"How could you betray me with a kiss?"

"Why do you arrest me here?"

"I am being treated like a criminal."

They led Jesus away.

Peter Lies about Knowing Jesus

Jesus was arrested and led away to the house of the high priest, while Peter followed at a distance. Some people built a fire in the middle of the courtyard and were sitting around it. Peter sat there with them, and a servant girl saw him. Then after she had looked at him carefully, she said, "This man was with Jesus!"

Peter said, "Woman, I don't even know that man!"

A little later someone else saw Peter and said, "You are one of them!"

"No, I'm not!" Peter replied.

About an hour later another man insisted, "This man must have been with Jesus. They both come from Galilee."

Peter replied, "I don't know what you are talking about!" Right then, while Peter was still speaking, a rooster crowed.

The Lord turned and looked at Peter. And Peter remembered that the Lord had said, "Before a rooster crows tomorrow morning, you will say three times that you don't know me." Then Peter went out and cried hard.

Based on Luke 22.54-62

Peter said, "Woman, I don't even know that man!"

Jesus was taken to the house of the high priest.

Peter warmed himself at a fire.

"He was a disciple of Jesus!"

"Woman, I don't know him."

"You are one of them!"

"No I am not!"

"This man was with Jesus in Galilee."

"I don't know what you are talking about."

Peter heard a rooster crow.

Jesus looked at Peter.

Peter remembered Jesus had said this would happen.

Jesus Dies on the Cross

Jesus and two criminals were led outside of Jerusalem to be put to death. When the soldiers came to the place called "The Skull," they nailed Jesus to a cross. They also nailed the two criminals to crosses, one on each side of Jesus.

Jesus said, "Father, forgive these people! They don't know what they're doing."

Around noon the sky turned dark and stayed that way until the middle of the afternoon. The sun stopped shining. Jesus shouted, "Father, I put myself in your hands!" Then he died.

When a Roman officer who was there saw what had happened, he praised God and said, "Jesus must really have been a good man!"

A crowd had gathered to see the terrible sight. Then after they had seen it, they felt brokenhearted and went home. All of Jesus' close friends and the women who had come with him from Galilee stood at a distance and watched.

Based on Luke 23.32-34, 44-49

Jesus said, "Father, forgive these people!
They don't know what they're doing."

Soldiers took Jesus to a hill.

They nailed Jesus to a cross.

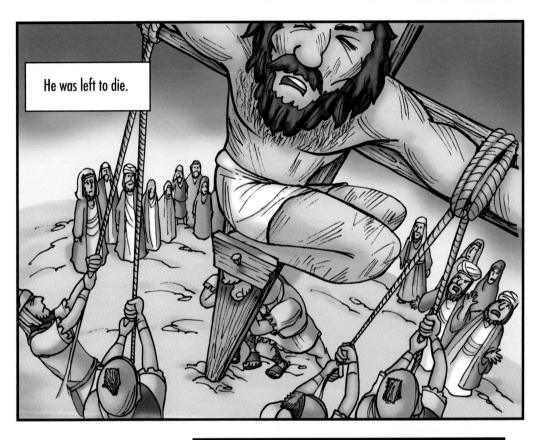

He was left to die.

"Please forgive these people for what they are doing."

Jesus Is Buried

There was a man named Joseph, who was from Judea. Joseph was a good and honest man, and he was eager for God's kingdom to come. He was also a member of the Jewish council, but he did not agree that Jesus was a criminal.

Joseph went to governor Pilate and asked for Jesus' body. He took the body down from the cross and wrapped it in fine cloth. Then he put Jesus' body in a tomb that had been cut out of solid rock. It was Friday, and the Sabbath was about to begin.

The women who had come with Jesus from Galilee followed Joseph and watched how Jesus' body was placed in the tomb. Then they went to prepare some sweet-smelling spices for his burial. But on the Sabbath they rested, as the Law of Moses commands.

Based on Luke 23.50-56

Joseph went to governor Pilate and asked for Jesus' body.

Joseph asked to bury Jesus.

Joseph took the body down from the cross.

He wrapped it in fine cloth.

Then Joseph carried the body...

and carefully laid it in a tomb.

Some followers of Jesus watched Joseph.

They left to prepare spices for the body.

Jesus Comes Alive

Very early on Sunday morning, after Jesus had died, a group of women went to the tomb where Jesus was buried. They were carrying the spices that they had prepared for the body. When they found the stone rolled away from the entrance, they went in. But they did not find the body of the Lord Jesus, and they did not know what to think.

Suddenly two men in shining white clothes stood beside them. The women were afraid and bowed to the ground. But the men said:

Why are you looking in the place of the dead for someone who is alive? Jesus isn't here! He has been raised from death. Remember that while he was still in Galilee, he told you, "The Son of Man will be handed over to sinners who will nail him to a cross. But three days later he will rise to life."

Then they remembered what Jesus had said.

Mary Magdalene, Joanna, Mary the mother of James, and some other women were the ones who had gone to the tomb. When they returned, they told the eleven apostles and the others what had happened. The apostles thought it was all nonsense, and they would not believe.

But Peter ran to the tomb. And when he stooped down and looked in, he saw only the burial clothes. Then he returned, wondering what had happened.

Based on Luke 24.1-12

KEY VERSE Luke 24.6

"Jesus isn't here! He has been raised from death."

Women came to prepare Jesus' body for burial.

They found the stone rolled away.

The women rushed to tell everyone.

"Jesus is alive!"

Peter ran to see for himself.

He saw the empty tomb and wondered what had happened.

Jesus Appears to Mary

Mary Magdalene stood crying outside the tomb. She was still weeping, when she saw two angels inside. They were dressed in white and were sitting where Jesus' body had been. One was at the head and the other was at the foot. The angels asked Mary, "Why are you crying?"

She answered, "They have taken away my Lord's body! I don't know where they have put him."

As soon as Mary said this, she turned around and saw Jesus standing there. But she did not know who he was. Jesus asked her, "Why are you crying? Who are you looking for?"

She thought he was the gardener and said, "Sir, if you have taken his body away, please tell me, so I can go and get him."

Then Jesus said to her, "Mary!"

She turned and said to him, "Rabboni." The Aramaic word "Rabboni" means "Teacher."

Jesus told her, "Don't hold on to me! I have not yet gone to the Father. But tell my disciples that I am going to the one who is my Father and my God, as well as your Father and your God." Mary Magdalene then went and told the disciples that she had seen the Lord. She also told them what he had said to her.

Based on John 20.11-18

Mary Magdalene then went and told the disciples that she had seen the Lord.

Mary Magdalene went to Jesus' tomb.

She saw two angels inside.

"Why are you crying?"

"Someone has taken Jesus' body away."

Mary did not recognize Jesus.

"Why are you crying?"

"Do you know where they have taken Jesus' body?"

"Mary, it's me."

"My teacher."

"Tell my disciples I am going to God the Father."

Jesus Appears to His Disciples

The disciples were gathered in a room when suddenly, Jesus appeared among them. He greeted them and showed them his hands and his side. When the disciples saw the Lord, they became very happy.

After Jesus had greeted them again, he said, "I am sending you, just as the Father has sent me." Then he breathed on them and said, "Receive the Holy Spirit. If you forgive anyone's sins, they will be forgiven. But if you don't forgive their sins, they will not be forgiven."

Although Thomas the Twin was one of the twelve disciples, he wasn't with the others when Jesus appeared to them. So they told him, "We have seen the Lord!"

But Thomas said, "First, I must see the nail scars in his hands and touch them with my finger. I must put my hand where the spear went into his side. I won't believe unless I do this!"

A week later the disciples were together again. This time, Thomas was with them. Jesus came in while the doors were still locked and stood in the middle of the group. He greeted his disciples and said to Thomas, "Put your finger here and look at my hands! Put your hand into my side. Stop doubting and have faith!"

Thomas replied, "You are my Lord and my God!"

Jesus said, "Thomas, do you have faith because you have seen me? The people who have faith in me without seeing me are the ones who are really blessed!"

Based on John 20.19-29

Jesus showed them
his hands and side.

They were happy
to see Jesus alive.

Several days later,
they told Thomas what
they had seen.

"I will not believe it
unless I see Jesus."

Suddenly Jesus appeared again.

He showed his scarred hands to Thomas.

"Blessed are those who will believe without seeing me."

Jesus Is Taken to Heaven

While the apostles were still with Jesus, they asked him, "Lord, are you now going to give Israel its own king again?"

Jesus said to them, "You don't need to know the time of those events that only the Father controls. But the Holy Spirit will come upon you and give you power. Then you will tell everyone about me in Jerusalem, in all Judea, in Samaria, and everywhere in the world." After Jesus had said this and while they were watching, he was taken up into a cloud. They could not see him, but as he went up, they kept looking up into the sky.

Suddenly two men dressed in white clothes were standing there beside them. They said, "Why are you men from Galilee standing here and looking up into the sky? Jesus has been taken to heaven. But he will come back in the same way that you have seen him go."

Based on Acts 1.6-11

While they were watching, Jesus was taken up into a cloud.

The disciples asked Jesus about Israel's future.

"Only God knows such things."

"Stay in Jerusalem and wait."

"The Holy Spirit will come and help you tell others about me."

Then Jesus was taken up into the clouds.

The disciples kept looking for him.

"Why are you looking for Jesus?"

"Jesus is in heaven, but he will return some day."

Good News in Different Languages

On the Jewish festival of Pentecost all the Lord's followers were together in one place. Suddenly there was a noise from heaven like the sound of a mighty wind! It filled the house where they were meeting. Then they saw what looked like fiery tongues moving in all directions, and a tongue came and settled on each person there. The Holy Spirit took control of everyone, and they began speaking whatever languages the Spirit let them speak.

Many religious Jews from every country in the world were living in Jerusalem. And when they heard this noise, a crowd gathered. But they were surprised, because they were hearing everything in their own languages.

They were excited and amazed, and said, "Don't all these who are speaking come from Galilee? Then why do we hear them speaking our very own languages? Some of us are from other countries. Some of us were born Jews, and others of us have chosen to be Jews. Yet we all hear them using our own languages to tell the wonderful things God has done."

Everyone was excited and confused. Some of them even kept asking each other, "What does all this mean?"

Based on Acts 2.1-12

The Holy Spirit took control of everyone, and they began speaking whatever languages the Spirit let them speak.

Jesus' followers were together.

Suddenly a strong wind filled the room.

Tongues of fire rested over each person.

The Holy Spirit took control and everyone started speaking different languages.

People from other countries heard what was happening.

"How are these people speaking in our languages?"

All were amazed to hear the good news about Jesus.

God is doing great things!

A Beggar Gets More Than Money

The time of prayer was about three o'clock in the afternoon, and Peter and John were going into the temple in Jerusalem. A man who had been born lame was being carried to the temple door. Each day he was placed beside this door, known as the Beautiful Gate. He sat there and begged from the people who were going in.

The man saw Peter and John entering the temple, and he asked them for money. But they looked straight at him and said, "Look up at us!"

The man stared at them and thought he was going to get something. But Peter said, "I don't have any silver or gold! But I will give you what I do have. In the name of Jesus Christ from Nazareth, get up and start walking." Peter then took him by the right hand and helped him up.

At once the man's feet and ankles became strong, and he jumped up and started walking. He went with Peter and John into the temple, walking and jumping and praising God. Everyone saw him walking around and praising God. They knew that he was the beggar who had been lying beside the Beautiful Gate, and they were completely surprised. They could not imagine what had happened to the man.

Based on Acts 3.1-10

*Peter said to the man, "In the name of
Jesus Christ from Nazareth, get up and start walking."*

Peter and John were
going to the temple.

"Can you please
give me money?"

"We have no money."

"But I will give you what I have," Peter said.

"In Jesus' name, stand up and walk."

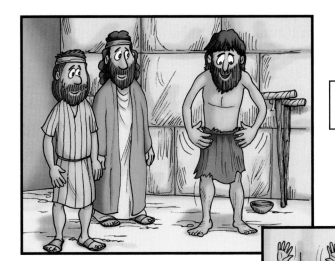

The man started walking.

He jumped up and
down praising God.

Everyone was surprised
to see the man walk.

Saul Meets Jesus

Saul kept on threatening to kill the Lord's followers. He even went to the high priest and asked for letters to Jewish leaders in Damascus. He did this because he wanted to arrest and take to Jerusalem any man or woman who had accepted the Lord's Way. When Saul had almost reached Damascus, a bright light from heaven suddenly flashed around him. He fell to the ground and heard a voice that said, "Saul! Saul! Why are you so cruel to me?"

"Who are you?" Saul asked.

"I am Jesus," the Lord answered. "I am the one you are so cruel to. Now get up and go into the city, where you will be told what to do."

The men with Saul stood there speechless. They had heard the voice, but they had not seen anyone. Saul got up from the ground, and when he opened his eyes, he could not see a thing. Someone then led him by the hand to Damascus, and for three days he was blind and did not eat or drink.

A follower named Ananias lived in Damascus, and the Lord spoke to him in a vision. Ananias answered, "Lord, here I am."

The Lord said to him, "Get up and go to the house of Judas on Straight Street. When you get there, you will find a man named Saul from the city of Tarsus. Saul is praying, and he has seen a vision. He saw a man named Ananias coming to him and putting his hands on him, so that he could see again."

Ananias left and went into the house where Saul was staying. Ananias placed his hands on him and said, "Saul, the Lord Jesus has sent me. He is the same one who appeared to you along the road. He wants you to be able to see and to be filled with the Holy Spirit.

Suddenly something like fish scales fell from Saul's eyes, and he could see. He got up and was baptized. Then he ate and felt much better.

Based on Acts 9.1-12, 17-19

Suddenly something like fish scales fell from Saul's eyes, and he could see.

Saul wanted to get rid of the followers of Jesus.

He went to Damascus to find them.

Suddenly a bright light blinded Saul.

"Saul, why are you cruel to me?"

"Who are you?"

"I am Jesus. Go to the city and wait for my instructions."

A follower of Jesus
came to visit Saul.

"The Lord has sent me
to heal you."

Saul could see again.

Paul and Silas in Prison

Soon after Saul began preaching about Jesus, his name was changed to Paul. One day he and his helper Silas were put in prison for what they taught.

About midnight Paul and Silas were praying and singing praises to God, while the other prisoners listened. Suddenly a strong earthquake shook the jail to its foundations. The doors opened, and the chains fell from all the prisoners.

When the jailer woke up and saw that the doors were open, he thought that the prisoners had escaped. He pulled out his sword and was about to kill himself. But Paul shouted, "Don't harm yourself! No one has escaped."

The jailer asked for a torch and went into the jail. He was shaking all over as he knelt down in front of Paul and Silas. After he had led them out of the jail, he asked, "What must I do to be saved?"

They replied, "Have faith in the Lord Jesus and you will be saved! This is also true for everyone who lives in your home."

Then Paul and Silas told him and everyone else in his house about the Lord. While it was still night, the jailer took them to a place where he could wash their cuts and bruises. Then he and everyone in his home were baptized. They were very glad that they had put their faith in God. After this, the jailer took Paul and Silas to his home and gave them something to eat.

Based on Acts 16.25-34

"Have faith in the Lord Jesus and you will be saved!"

Paul and Silas were praying.

An earthquake caused the prison doors to open.

The jailor feared that all the prisoners had escaped!

"Everyone is still here."

"What must I do to be saved?"

"Have faith in Jesus."

The jailer believed
and told his family.

Then they also
believed in Jesus.

Paul Preaches in Rome

Paul was sent to Rome as a prisoner for teaching about Jesus. He was allowed to live in a house with a soldier to guard him. One day, he met with the local Jewish leaders and told them:

My friends, I have never done anything to hurt our people, and I have never gone against the customs of our ancestors. But in Jerusalem I was handed over as a prisoner to the Romans. They looked into the charges against me and wanted to release me. They found that I had not done anything deserving death. The Jewish leaders disagreed, so I asked to be tried by the Emperor. But I don't have anything to say against my own nation.

For two years Paul stayed in a rented house and welcomed everyone who came to see him. He bravely preached about God's kingdom and taught about the Lord Jesus Christ, and no one tried to stop him.

Based on Acts 28.17-19, 30, 31

Paul bravely preached about God's kingdom
and taught about the Lord Jesus Christ.

Paul was taken to Rome as a prisoner.

Paul was guarded by a soldier.

"I am not here to hurt anyone."

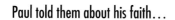

Paul told them about his faith…

and everything that happened to him.

Paul taught everyone about Jesus.

Nothing Keeps Us from God's Love

Paul in his preaching to the Romans said:

If God is on our side, can anyone be against us? God did not keep back his own Son, but he gave him for us. If God did this, won't he freely give us everything else? If God says his chosen ones are acceptable to him, can anyone bring charges against them?

Or can anyone condemn them? No indeed! Christ died and was raised to life, and now he is at God's right side, speaking to him for us. Can anything separate us from the love of Christ? Can trouble, suffering, and hard times, or hunger and nakedness, or danger and death?

In everything we have won more than a victory because of Christ who loves us. I am sure that nothing can separate us from God's love—not life or death, not angels or spirits, not the present or the future, and not powers above or powers below. Nothing in all creation can separate us from God's love for us in Christ Jesus our Lord!

Based on Romans 8.31-39

Nothing in all creation can separate us from God's love for us in Christ Jesus our Lord!

Paul said, "God loves us and sent Jesus to be with us."

God's love helps us face our enemies.

Trouble and danger cannot stop God's love.

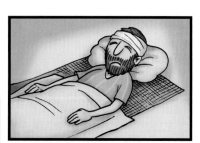

God's love goes with us into the future.

Evil powers cannot
keep God's love away.

Nothing keeps us from God's love.

Each Gift Is Important

Paul offers advice to Christians:

The body of Christ has many different parts, just as any other body does. Some of us are Jews, and others are Gentiles. Some of us are slaves, and others are free. But God's Spirit baptized each of us and made us part of the body of Christ. Now we each drink from that same Spirit.

Our bodies don't have just one part. They have many parts. Suppose a foot says, "I'm not a hand, and so I'm not part of the body." Wouldn't the foot still belong to the body? Or suppose an ear says, "I'm not an eye, and so I'm not part of the body." Wouldn't the ear still belong to the body? If our bodies were only an eye, we couldn't hear a thing. And if they were only an ear, we couldn't smell a thing. But God has put all parts of our body together in the way that he decided is best.

Together you are the body of Christ. Each one of you is part of his body. First, God chose some people to be apostles and prophets and teachers for the church. But God also chose some to work miracles or heal the sick or help others or be leaders or speak different kinds of languages. Not everyone is an apostle. Not everyone is a prophet. Not everyone is a teacher. Not everyone can work miracles. Not everyone can heal the sick. Not everyone can speak different kinds of languages.

Based on 1 Corinthians 12.12-18, 27-30

Together you are the body of Christ.

The world has many
different people.

Every person is important to God.

Some people teach.

Others pray for the sick.

Some are leaders.

Others speak different languages.

Everyone's gifts are needed.

A New Way of Living

Paul wrote these words to Christians:

I beg you to live in a way that is worthy of the people God has chosen to be his own. Always be humble and gentle. Patiently put up with each other and love each other. Try your best to let God's Spirit keep your hearts united. Do this by living at peace.

We are part of the same body. Stop lying and start telling each other the truth. Don't get so angry that you sin. Don't go to bed angry and don't give the devil a chance.

If you are a thief, quit stealing. Be honest and work hard, so you will have something to give to people in need.

Stop all your dirty talk. Say the right thing at the right time and help others by what you say.

Don't make God's Spirit sad. The Spirit makes you sure that some day you will be free from your sins.

Stop being bitter and angry and mad at others. Don't yell at one another or curse each other or ever be rude. Instead, be kind and merciful, and forgive others, just as God forgave you because of Christ.

Based on Ephesians 4.1-3, 25-32

Be kind and merciful, and forgive others.

Always be kind.

Live at peace with others.

Don't get so angry that you hurt someone.

Never steal.

Only say kind things.

Give to those in need.

Don't yell at anyone.

Forgive others.

Jesus Will Come Back

John wrote down the vision he had about Jesus:

I saw a new heaven and a new earth. The first heaven and the first earth had disappeared, and so had the sea. Then I saw New Jerusalem, that holy city, coming down from God in heaven. It was like a bride dressed in her wedding gown and ready to meet her husband.

I heard a loud voice shout from the throne:

God's home is now with his people. He will live with them, and they will be his own. Yes, God will make his home among his people. He will wipe all tears from their eyes, and there will be no more death, suffering, crying, or pain. These things of the past are gone forever.

Then I was told:

These words are true and can be trusted. The Lord God controls the spirits of his prophets, and he is the one who sent his angel to show his servants what must happen right away. Remember, I am coming soon! God will bless everyone who pays attention to the message of this book.

Based on Revelation 21.1-4; 22.6,7

Jesus said, "Remember, I am coming soon!"

John had a vision.

He saw a new heaven and earth and New Jerusalem.

MY READING TOOLBOX

Words To Remember

Words To Remember is a list of important words you will come across in **Bible Now!** Use this list like a dictionary to look up and remember the words you read.

agreement In the Bible, this usually refers to the special promises (or covenants) God made with the people of Israel.

altar A raised place where sacrifices and offerings were made to God. Altars were usually made of stones (either rough or smooth), packed earth, or pottery.

Assyria (uh-**sihr**-ee-uh) A nation northeast of Israel. Assyria was an enemy of Israel. Assyria can be found on the map "Places in the Ancient World."

Babylonia (bab-uh-**loh**-nee-uh) A nation northeast of Israel. Babylonia was Israel's enemy who defeated Jerusalem and took the people away as prisoners. Babylonia can be found on the map "Places in the Ancient World."

baptize, baptism A word that means "to dip in water." Followers of Jesus were baptized to show they had made a decision to live the way Jesus had taught them.

blessing A promise of something good that will happen, usually good health, lots of children, or a long life. A blessing comes from God or from another person.

Canaan (**kay**-nuhn) The name of the land where the people of Israel settled. In the Bible, Canaan is often called the Promised Land. It was later called Israel. Canaan can be found on the map "Places in the Ancient World."

curse A promise that something very bad will happen, usually sickness, dying, bad weather, or war. In the Bible, God cursed people who lived their own way and not God's way.

Cyrus (**seye**-ruhs) A king of Persia who let the people of Israel return home after living as prisoners in Babylonia.

descendant (dee-**sen**-duhnt) The family members (like children, grandchildren, and great-grandchildren) who live after a certain person. In the Bible, the Israelites are considered the descendants of Abraham and Sarah.

Words To Remember

Egypt (**ee**-jipt) A nation southwest of Israel. Egypt was the place where the Israelites lived as slaves. Moses led them out of Egypt to freedom. Egypt can be found on the map "Places in the Ancient World."

Galilee (**gal**-uh-lee) The northern region of Palestine. Jesus often traveled and taught about God in cities located in Galilee. Galilee can be found on the map "Places Jesus Knew."

Hebrew Another name for the people of Israel. Hebrew is also the name of the language they spoke. Most of the Old Testament was originally written in Hebrew.

Holy Spirit God's spirit that works on earth. God's spirit gave life to humans and animals at creation. Later, the Holy Spirit came to give Jesus' disciples the power to tell everyone the Good News about Jesus.

idol (**eye**-duhl) A statue or image of a god that people worship. People living in the ancient world worshiped many different idols, but God's Law commanded the Israelites not to make or worship any idol.

Israel (**iz**-ray-uhl) God's special people, and the name of the nation where they lived. Kings Saul, David, and Solomon all ruled over the nation of Israel. Israel is the land located between the Mediterranean Sea and the Jordan River on the map "Places in the Old Testament."

Israelite (**iz**-ray-uh-lite) A descendant of Jacob, the grandson of Abraham. Another name for a Hebrew.

Jerusalem (ji-**roo**-suh-luhm) The capital city of Israel. Jerusalem is located a little north and west of the Dead Sea on the map "Places in the Old Testament."

Judah (**joo**-duh) The name of the southern kingdom after the nation of Israel was divided into two separate kingdoms.

Kingdom of Heaven A way to describe God's rule over people on earth.

Words To Remember

Law of Moses God's laws and instructions for right living. God gave these laws to Moses for the people of Israel.

Lord A name for the God of Israel. Later, the disciples called Jesus Lord.

Mount of Olives A hill east of Jerusalem good for growing olives. Jesus prayed there just before he was arrested in Jerusalem.

Nazareth (**naz**-uh-rith) The small city in Galilee where Jesus grew up. Nazareth can be found on the map "Places Jesus Knew."

Nebuchadnezzar (neb-uh-kuhd-**nez**-uhr) The name of a powerful king of Babylonia who ruled 605–562 B.C. It was Nebuchadnezzar II who defeated the kingdom of Judah, destroyed Jerusalem, and took the people away as prisoners.

offering Something given to God in worship, usually an animal, money, olive oil, or grain. Offerings were used to honor or to give thanks to God.

Palestine The name used to refer to Israel during New Testament times. Palestine is the land located between the Mediterranean Sea and the Jordan River on the map "Places Jesus Knew."

Passover The Jewish festival that celebrates the escape of the Hebrew people from slavery in Egypt. Jesus and his followers celebrated Passover, and it is still celebrated today in late March or early April.

Pharisees (**fair**-uh-sees) A Jewish religious group during the days of Jesus. The Pharisees carefully obeyed every word of the Law of Moses.

Philistines (**fi**-lis-teens) A violent people who settled in the southern coast of Canaan as early as the twelfth century B.C. The Philistines were constant enemies of Israel.

priest A person who served in the temple by overseeing the worship of God and the offerings that were made there.

Words To Remember

prophet (**prof**-fut) A spokesperson who receives a message directly from God and repeats it to people. Elijah, Isaiah, Ezekiel, and Zephaniah were some of Israel's prophets.

Rabbi (**rab**-eye) A Hebrew word that means "my teacher." Some of Jesus' followers called him Rabbi.

sacred chest The wooden box (or Ark) that held the stone tablets with the Ten Commandments written on them. The sacred chest traveled with the Hebrew people from Egypt to Canaan, and was later put in the temple.

sacrifice (**sack**-ruh-fice) An animal, fruit, or grain offering that was burned on an altar to honor God or to ask God for a blessing or forgiveness.

sin Turning away from God and acting in ways that are opposed to God's teaching.

Sinai (**seye**-neye) The holy mountain where God gave Moses the Ten Commandments and other laws for the people of Israel. Sinai is also the name of the desert the people traveled through from Egypt to Canaan.

temple A sacred building used as a place of worship. In the Bible, the word usually refers to God's temple in Jerusalem.

tomb (toom) A place where a body was buried. In the time of Jesus, tombs were usually cut out of a rocky hillside. A large flat stone was used to close off the opening to the tomb.

tribe A large group of people who had a common ancestor. The tribe was made up of several clans, which were made up of several families.

worship To express devotion or loyalty to God. Worship usually involves prayer and the singing of praises to God. In the Old Testament, sacrifices were also a part of worshiping God.

People To Remember

People To Remember is a list of the most important people mentioned in **Bible Now!**
Use this list to find the pages where you can read about them in **Bible Now!**

People To Remember

Topics To Remember

Topics To Remember is a tool that lists some of the important topics found in the stories of **Bible Now!** Look through the list and find a topic that you want to read about, then turn to the pages in **Bible Now!** to read that story.

Topics To Remember

Scriptures To Remember

Scriptures To Remember is a list of all the Bible passages found in **Bible Now!**
Use this list to look up a Scripture and find the pages where you can read it in
Bible Now!

Old Testament

Scripture To Remember

Places To Remember

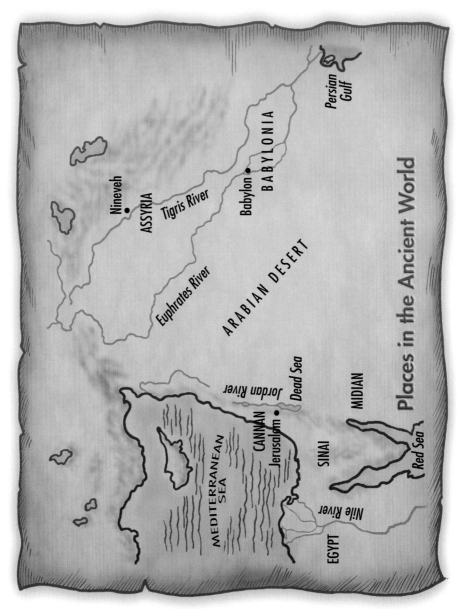

Places in the Ancient World

Persian
Gulf

Nineveh

ASSYRIA

Tigris River

Babylon

BABYLONIA

Euphrates River

ARABIAN DESERT

Dead Sea

Jordan River

MIDIAN

CANAAN

Jerusalem

SINAI

MEDITERRANEAN
SEA

Red Sea

Nile River

EGYPT

Places To Remember

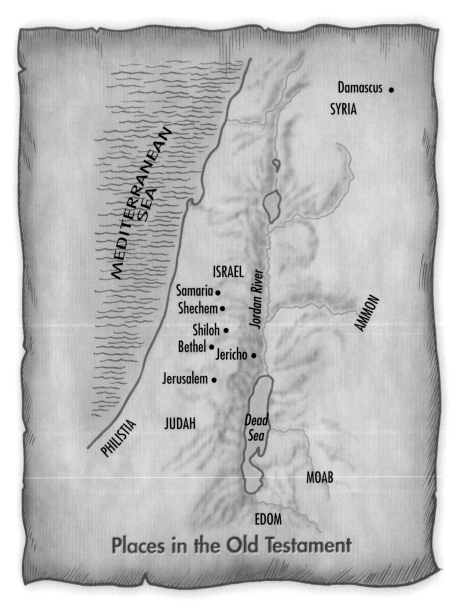

Places in the Old Testament

Places To Remember

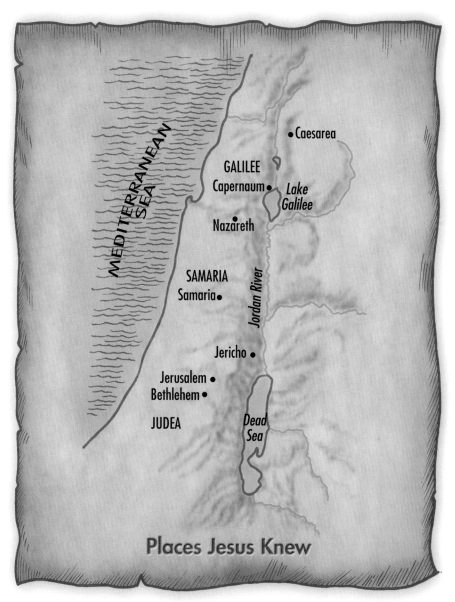

Places Jesus Knew

Places To Remember

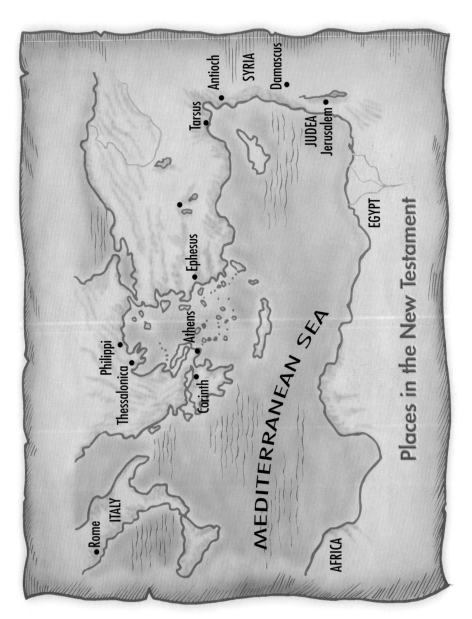

SYRIA

Antioch

Damascus

Tarsus

JUDEA

Jerusalem

EGYPT

Ephesus

Athens

MEDITERRANEAN SEA

Philippi

Thessalonica

Corinth

Places in the New Testament

ITALY

Rome

AFRICA